John Paul Egbert

Some Lessons from the Parable of the Sower, the Parable of Growth and the Law of the Harvest

John Paul Egbert

Some Lessons from the Parable of the Sower, the Parable of Growth and the Law of the Harvest

ISBN/EAN: 9783744762281

Printed in Europe, USA, Canada, Australia, Japan

Cover: Foto ©Lupo / pixelio.de

More available books at **www.hansebooks.com**

SOME LESSONS

FROM THE

PARABLE OF THE SOWER

THE

PARABLE OF GROWTH

AND THE

LAW OF THE HARVEST

By J. P. EGBERT.

BUFFALO
ULBRICH & KINGSLEY
1886

PREFACE.

A pastor often feels with pain the weakness of his work, and seeks to find some means to increase its value.

It is with this desire to strengthen a consciously defective ministry that these studies of "the Word of the Kingdom" have been prepared.

First delivered as sermons in Calvary Church, they were then written out from the stenographer's notes, and are published as nearly as possible as they were delivered.

The pleasure of their preparation has been increased by the thought that perhaps

PREFACE.

they may carry true seed to some "good and honest" heart, or help the growth to fuller harvest of seed already sown. Should this be accomplished, it may justify the addition of one more to the many books that ask for our attention. If it find no ministry of helpfulness, it will at least do no harm to those who take the time to read it.

As we are all stewards of the truth, do not forget to ask for the blessing of the God of all truth upon whatever in this little book is according to His Word.

STUDY OF CALVARY CHURCH.

May, 1886.

CONTENTS.

	PAGE.
Teaching by Parables．．．．．．．．．．．．．．．．．．．．．．．．．．．．．．	1
The Parable of the Sower．．．．．．．．．．．．．．．．．．．．．．．．．．．	37
The First Class, " By the Wayside "．．．．．．．．．．．．．	49
The Second Class, " On the Rock "．．．．．．．．．．．．．．	65
The Third Class, " Among Thorns "．．．．．．．．．．．．．	83
The Fourth Class, " In Good Ground "．．．．．．．．．．	106
" Take Heed How Ye Hear"．．．．．．．．．．．．．．．．．．．．．．．．	123
Parable of Growth．．．．．．．．．．．．．．．．．．．．．．．．．．．．．．．．．．	134
The Law of the Harvest．．．．．．．．．．．．．．．．．．．．．．．．．．．．	174

"...... the Holy Scriptures, which are able to make thee wise unto salvation."   —*II Tim.*, 3:15.

"...... Ask not for a sign from Heaven,
In the gospel of thy Saviour, life as well as light, is given.
Ever looking unto Jesus, all his glory thou shalt see,
From thy heart the veil be taken, and the Word be clear to thee."   —*De Wette.*

"Voice of the Holy Spirit, making known
Man to himself, a witness swift and sure,
Warning, approving, true and wise and pure,
Counsel and guidance that misleadeth none!
By thee the mystery of life is read;
The picture-writing of the world's gray seers,
The myths and parables of the primal years,
Whose letter kills, by thee interpreted
Take healthful meanings fitted to our needs,
And in the soul's vernacular, express
The common law of simple righteousness."
  —*J. G. Whittier.*

TEACHING BY PARABLES.

"*Why speakest thou to them in parables?*"

This question of the disciples suggests a line of thought which may be profitable to us as an introduction to the parables of our Lord, especially to the Parable of the Sower.

The great Teacher did not use parables for their beauty, nor chiefly for their power as illustrations. They are rather hints of something deeper; surface indications of richer ore beneath, for which we must dig watchfully and thoroughly. And we may be sure that parables meant more to Christ than they do to us. As the botanist walking through the forest sees a variety and wealth of which the woodman never dreams; or as the anthropologist, looking at the common customs of men, sees a far-reaching history with a wealth of meaning that is never more than a surface suggestion to the mass of men; so the Christ, "by whom all things consist," sees nature's secrets in all their infinite depth of meaning.

Where we see the conflicts that keep nature's surface in agitation, He sees the perfect concord reigning deep within. Behind the infinite variety that puzzles us, and the struggle of forces that bewilders us, He reads the eternal purpose of God blending all into the most perfect harmony. His pure eyes see a wealth to which our eyes are blind, and His mighty hand draws it forth for the world's instruction. Divine Himself, He is conscious of the divine knowledge and beauty written in with every scroll of nature. So that where all looks dark and deadly to us, He sees a divine truth, the truth of Jehovah's certain purpose, relieving with its own glory all the seeming defects and contradictions of earth. It adds to the value as well as to the beauty of the gospel message, that the Christ Teacher wove it into such close relations with all the works of God, among which we must delve for our daily life.

The Teacher who knew what was in man, knew also what was in nature, and taught us how to take more than a mere glance at the vast gallery of truth and beauty through which we are passing. He taught us to look for Jehovah's thought in every problem of nature, and to listen for the Father's voice of love and wisdom in every incident of life. He would have us search every nook of earthly life for the footprints of divine purpose, for the incarnation of divine thought, for the illustration of divine truth. To Him all things in the heavens and the earth, in the fields, the sea and the air, were filled with the thoughts of the eternal Mind, and He interpreted them into current language for circulation through all the years of human life. These truths He would force into the consciousness of men, and by them arouse us to an earnest effort to reach His own high standard for us.

On the head, the arm, the foot, you

touch the throbbing pulse, and think of the heart that beats its life-strokes into every part of the body. As the divine Teacher touches the pulses of truth, beating their mysterious harmonies everywhere throughout all life, He points our minds to the great Unity, who, like an eternal heart, sends a mighty intimation of His plan and presence throbbing through all the veins of nature. Thus He would lead us to search beyond the discord for the eternal harmony toward which He is leading us.

You may thus at last learn that

> "All nature is but art unknown to thee ;
> All chance, direction which thou canst not see ;
> All discord, harmony not understood ;
> All partial evil, universal good."—*Pope.*

Without doubt, he is the richest heir of God who has most familiarity with the divine meanings of nature; and that lover of nature is truest and happiest who can discern in her teachings the truths of God's implanting. As such a student looks on nature's problems, he is often forced to ask the question of the angel in Milton :—

> "What if earth
> Be but the shadow of Heaven and things therein,
> Each to other like more than on earth is thought?"

Certainly the Master used the earthly to teach us of things heavenly. For however others may read nature, Christ teaches that this world is a divine thought, God's world; and that men are the highest part of that thought, a copy of the Divine Thinker; and that many of the mysteries that fall like shadows across the world are but intimations of Jehovah's presence. Earth's treasures of truth are being discovered more and more richly every year by this eager, busy age, and science has given us many keys that unlock her secrets, yet her meaning is continually misinterpreted and her instructions misapplied. As we rejoice over earth's wealth and beauty, we do not always realize how true it is that

> "The earth is crammed with Heaven,
> And every bush afire with God."

Men are constantly saying the world is full of prophecies and man is full of hopes, but where is the promise of their fulfillment? The Word, the supreme Thought incarnate, comes to lighten man's darkness, to lift the world's hopes still higher by the divine assurance, to point man's limited, hindered, heavy-laden life to the rest of perfection, the unhindered growth of eternal life. Though all the world groaneth and travaileth until now, the time of rest comes rapidly, when all the hidden things of the universe will reveal their meaning. When we shall live amid great thoughts and holy purposes, amid our highest hopes fulfilled, and higher hopes begotten. When the natural and the spiritual shall build each other into symmetry, and by Christ's teaching shall reveal each other to the instruction and the comfort of all who listen to His voice.

The Master ever interprets nature as speaking the truth of God. The mountain points to the sure refuge in Jehovah's strength and protection, the rock illustrates His abiding salvation. The lily in its beauty, and the birds in the free air above, point to God's providing care. The golden grain drops into the fertile earth and springs up to a more abundant life, and the seeds of divine truth fall into the "good and honest" heart only to spring up into the abundance of eternal life.

"Go to the earth," says Job, "and it shall teach thee," and the Psalmist continues the song, "for the earth is the Lord's and the fulness thereof." (Ps. 24: 1.) "O Lord, how manifold are Thy works! in wisdom hast Thou made them all: the earth is full of Thy riches." (Ps. 104: 24.) God has summoned all the resources of the whole realm of nature to aid in the upbuilding of man; and from the open pages of this visible universe Christ has taught us to read the truths of the unseen and eternal world. He so mingled the visible world about Him with the unseen world of His promise as to make the unseen things more real by association with things we knew. He read such divine truth from the suggestions of nature, and made the present mean so much by its relations with the eternal future; so unveiled that future by showing the real meaning of the present, and so rifted the cloud that separated them, as to make them forever stand forth as to-day and to-morrow of the same immortal life. Thus teaching us that the present is the parable of the unbounded future, and only as we rightly read the days that are, can we understand the years that shall be.

How patiently Christ battled with the world's darkness, shining like the rising sun against the world's clouds and fogs of sin and error, striving to make Heaven's glorious light scatter every human darkness. Earnestly, longingly, did He labor to fill men's minds with thoughts of God, and put into their souls His own high aim of life. The Parable of the Sower suggests the manner in which the world receives His earnest teaching.

The disciples appear to have been surprised by this parable. Not so much that He spake in parables, but that He used parables at this time and to this people. They are not very sure that they understand His meaning in the parable just uttered; but if they do, why does this Teacher, so earnest and so wise, speak such a parable to such an audience? It is not an illustration of God's love and mercy. It is not an exhibition of Christ's divine mission to our fallen race. As one has said, "He preached not to the people, but at them, or over their heads." No comforting truth of revelation, but a discouraging, heart-searching analysis of the characters of His hearers. It was not a gospel message, but an uncomfortable, depressing statement of how the gospel would be received.

That listening assembly was made up of a few who believed, and a multitude who were either indifferent, save from mere curiosity, or were prejudiced against Him, some even hating Him with a readiness to kill Him. Why did not Christ use this opportunity for a parable illustrating the grandeur of His mission, or the infinite greatness of His Father's love? How appropriate the parable of the "Prodigal Son," or the "Lost Sheep," or the "Pearl of Great Price." Instead of any vindication of Himself, or any propitiation of His hearers, He speaks to them a parable that, if understood, will discourage many, and rouse more to wrath that may seek to compass His own destruction. Why lose this fine opportunity for a sermon on the great truths of God's heavenly kingdom, or an earnest presentation of the Father's infinite love and mercy? How little we see of things that are clear to the Master's vision!

The disciples might easily have been deceived, as we often are, into thinking that the multitude would press into the heavenly kingdom if only the gospel were appropriately preached unto them. These eager followers, who yet judge by appearances, dread to hear a word that might drive away the large audiences, or check their enthusiasm. But Christ preached not merely to the senses. That audience was much better understood by Christ than by the disciples, and from His perfect knowledge of the human heart He would take a lesson for the continual use of His disciples, and of all who preach His word.

The crowd was very great, "There was gathered unto him a great multitude," coming "out of every city," along that thickly populated lake-shore, and filled with eagerness to hear the wonderful words of the new prophet. The enthusiasm would have gladdened the heart of any human teacher, yet Christ speaks to the crowd a parable that carries a sad strain in almost every sentence. The disciples were disappointed, yet they were curious to know their Master's purpose.

"Why speakest thou to them in parables?" "What might this parable mean?"

They had yet but little experience of their Teacher's ways, and were only beginning to understand His mission among them. They had not learned, and how few of us have learned, to wait patiently with a sure confidence that He who spake as never man speaks, has spoken with unerring wisdom.

He knows that in a few days, when He forces the real nature of His mission on their dull hearts, that crowd will scatter to all distances from Him, some even to do their part in hastening His condemnation. He sees the whole field of living souls before Him divided into the four classes He describes in the parable, and in deep sadness utters what He so certainly knows and so keenly feels. How few are the real members of His divine kingdom, and what a crowd of eager seekers after sensations!

The Saviour's reply tells how He understood the question of His little school of disciples. "Therefore speak I to them in parables; because seeing they see not, and hearing they hear not, neither do they understand." Over that soil He has sown the pure seed of divine truth, yet all their thoughts are carnal. *"In them is fulfilled the prophecy of Isaiah, which saith, By hearing ye shall hear, and shall not understand; and seeing ye shall see, and shall not perceive: for this people's heart is waxed gross, and their ears are dull of hearing, and their eyes they have closed; lest at any time they should see with their eyes, and hear with their ears, and should understand with their heart, and should be converted, and I should heal them."* They see and hear, but their hearts are become so gross and foul that they cannot understand, or they would be converted. What a fearful sentence to pronounce upon any class of human beings, and yet how true! He sees in that crowd the fulfillment of the prophecy of Isaiah, and He prophesies a result soon to be apparent to all. The enthusiasm is at its height, and a vast multitude is eager to make Him king; but in a few days He will enter Capernaum, and to the same multitude, with increase, He will preach that wonderful sermon on the Bread of Life, after which the whole Galilean revival seemed to collapse in almost total failure.

In this parable of the Sower, Christ says to all in that crowd who understand him, "Examine yourselves, and make sure of your own position, for in a few days I will pour a flood of light upon the real truth I came to teach, that will blind those who are still filled with the gross darkness of ignorance and unbelief; and at the same time I will also make clearer the boundaries of My heavenly kingdom—one class of you will be within the kingdom, many classes without. To which class do you belong?"

To His disciples He would say—"judge not by appearance, but learn well the lesson of this parable, for it is the judgment of omniscience upon every audience you will have to teach." Their own high, and not very clear, expectations might easily lead them to put too great a value upon the eagerness and enthusiasm of the increasing crowd. He bids them look deeper. For their instruction, He analyzes the very hearts of that listening congregation, and shows how few of them are "good and honest" soil in which truth can grow. It is an infinitely sad thought. Not only that many of them will not receive the truth, but cannot. Their hearts are too barren, or too thorny. They have lost their capacity to receive the truth with understanding. Was this more true then than now? Are there not multitudes now whose hearts are so gross as to make it impossible for spiritual truth to enter and abide?

No longer can those who catch the meaning of the parable be entirely unmindful of the high and unselfish purpose of their teacher; nor can they be altogether blind to the grossness and insincerity of the great congregations that listened to Him.

His interpretation of the parable is an evident revelation of His own omniscience, and a clear exhibition of His position as a teacher from God. At the same time it is an impressive lesson to His disciples upon the great necessity for the possession of a right spirit in order to understand all parables, and rightly judge all congregations. The Parable of the Sower has been to all Christ's followers an important, though sometimes very discouraging, lesson. The hard experiences of centuries have vividly illustrated and proven true these words of Him who "knew what was in man," and no longer can a teacher of truth speak to any audience without the thought that here, too, are the four classes of hearers. It is the handwriting of God upon every assembly listening to the gospel message. A few will hear the truth and treasure it in good and honest hearts, but the other classes are the more numerous. "Having ears they hear not." All who hear are modified by the truth, but how few are sanctified by it! Is it not strange and sorrowful that so few receive the truth into hearts all ready for its fullest growth, when the reward of knowing God is eternal life?

Many loudly-applauded philanthropic

schemes to reform the world have had a sudden success that deceived men into a temporary belief that they were divinely true, but their false interpretation of God, and their blindness to the narrowness, the hardness, and the thorny condition of our sinful hearts, have caused them to pass away as visions in the night, leaving the world still unreformed. But no follower of Christ, however enthusiastic for the world's redemption, can for a moment leave out of account the sin-disturbed vision, and sin-deadened ears of our degenerate souls. He ever remembers that "the servant is not greater than his Lord" even in this, and if they would not hear the Master they are not likely to hear the disciple. If from the hand of the divine Sower the seed fell into but few hearts that were "honest and good," the disciple may expect, without discouragement, that while he must "sow beside all waters," only here and there will there be a harvest.

Yet all true disciples of Christ work for His kingdom under the dominance of the ever present hope of its full success. "Thy kingdom come," is their earnest prayer, but it is also a loyal acceptance of their Master's prophecy that "the gospel of the kingdom shall be preached in the whole world." It is not their dream, it is not any mere scheme of reformation, but a steady, determined sowing of the "word of the kingdom," the fruit of which is ever good, and which would make this world all fruitful of heavenly graces if all hearts were but "good and honest." It is the seed of love, the foundation of all true and abiding philanthropy. Yet, if there were no promise of success, but only the command to sow, every true disciple would work with all diligence because it is the will of his Lord.

The disciples very evidently feel that Christ has thoughts deeper than the mere literal meaning of the parable, and they ask for the interpretation. He answers with a very suggestive question, "Know ye not this parable, how then will ye know all parables?" What, not understand so simple a parable as this? How then will ye understand the deeper parables which teach of Jehovah's nature and man's eternal future? This may be the meaning of His question, but does it not go deeper? Does it not reach down to the innermost spirit of every listener? The Christ might stand before this congregation and say, "I show you the Father?" and we answer, "only show us the Father and it sufficeth us." "What," he says, "have I been so long time with you, and yet hast thou not known Me? He that hath seen Me hath seen the Father." The fault is not in Him, it is not in God; it is in our hearts. The "pure in heart shall see God." Likeness is essential to perfect understanding. No man can have any clear insight into that with which he has no sympathy.

As Hartley Coleridge says: "Sympathy is the ground of mutual understanding." Or as Wordsworth so beautifully expresses it: "You must love Him ere to you He seem worthy of your love."

> "Whate'er we look on, at our side
> Be charity—to bid us think,
> And feel, if we would know."

Irving, in his Columbus, Bk. 7, ch. 1, first paragraph, gives a perfect illustration of this necessity of sympathy in order to understanding. It is a necessity always, but especially in spiritual matters.

The doubting Thomas cannot see the glorious meaning of the Christ life; but the new-born Thomas bows humbly, and with the very heart says, "My Lord and my God."

Apply this to that audience listening to the parable as Christ first utters it. Gross of heart, stubborn and blind, how could they understand a spiritual parable? "Their mood is for revolution, but not of their own lives." They would make Jesus a king, but not in their souls, nor according to the idea of His spiritual kingdom. They are full of enthusiasm for a miracle-worker who can feed them with loaves and fishes, but where is their zeal for truth, or loving, patient endurance for righteousness sake?

About one-half of Christ's earthly ministry is gone. He has scattered the seeds of truth broadcast over many great audiences. In spring-time, when hearts were opened with need and expectation, with divine skill He had sown the good seed "beside all waters." Not in parables, but in plain speech. Not in similitudes, but in the concise, startling, enduring beatitudes. His hearers saw His mighty deeds, but saw not their meaning or purpose. They heard His wonderful teachings, but caught not their life-giving value. "Seeing, they see not; hearing, they hear not." Now, as he wraps His thoughts in parable, those who understand may see the truth more clearly by the dress in which it is clothed, and in which those who have hardened themselves into grossness of heart may find their own judgment. Some went up into clearer light; the many went down into deeper darkness. Yet even as these "despisers of the word" went lower and lower, the familiar parable would cling to their memories, and might even yet challenge their attention to its hidden truths. As Von Gerlach says: "A parable is like the pillar of cloud and fire, which turned the dark side to the Egyptians, the bright side to the people of the covenant; it is like a shell which keeps the precious kernel as well for the diligent as from the indolent." When they would not hear the plain warnings and commands, when through grossness of heart they could not take hold of His spiritual promises, Christ gave the divine message in parables in order that, if possible, some of them might even yet perceive the deeper meaning within and be saved. Christ does not abandon them when they reject His message, but continues always to preach to them the word of life "And with many such parables spake He the word unto them, as they were able to hear it : and without a parable spake He not unto them; but privately to His own disciples He expounded all things."

But may we not catch a glimpse of the feeling in the heart of the Teacher as He uttered this parable, and thus see still more clearly its deeper meaning? Complained of, upbraided, misunderstood; selfish motives ascribed to His pure deeds, isolated, without sympathy, without the confidence of those He came to save; charged with crime by those for whom He would die; sorrowing unto death with the knowledge of human sinfulness; thus out of a heart so familiar with grief, He utters this parable. It was His omniscient view of the gigantic struggle now begun between truth from God and human sinfulness. Is it any wonder that He spake this parable in sadness? This was His prophecy concerning the reception of the truth, and all the history of Christianity is the fulfillment of His word. His infinite longing to save His people from the tyranny of sin, and from its final awful fruits; His immeasurable love for human souls; His divine enthusiasm for the truth, could not dim His vision to the reality of the wilful rejection by men of His sublimest efforts.

Infinitely sad, yet certainly true, is this

parable; and as true to-day as when Christ stood in the boat on Galilee's lake so long ago   And thus the record of Christ's own experience as a teacher became a prophecy of the experience of every teacher of truth so long as men remain the willing slaves of sin.

With what meaning and power this parable must have come to His disciples when, in later days, they tried to put spiritual truths into sensual and selfish hearts! They are to preach the gospel of love and peace to just such audiences as this now before the Saviour, and it is all important that they should know, not only the truth as it is represented in Jesus, but also the characters of their hearers, and the reception the word of truth will meet. They are eager, believing followers, but as yet only half understanding the great mission for which their Teacher is preparing them. Even long after this they were sorely vexed and surprised at their own lack of success. How soon and how thoroughly they learned what needs no illustration now, that the hearts of men are not inclined towards the truth as it is revealed in Jesus!

The answer to the question of the disciples may be further gathered from Christ's words in Mark 4,: 11. "Unto you it is given to know the mysteries of the kingdom of God: but to them that are without, all things are done in parables." This suggests a definite design for parables in relation to the "Kingdom of God." To those within the kingdom, suggesting truth and illustrating it for their upbuilding; to those without the kingdom, leaving a possibility that in the imagery some soul may catch a view of the truth, and be led to fuller knowledge. Christ's great mission on earth was to establish this kingdom in all the hearts of men. They had revolted, and become subjects of another king, the "Prince of this world." They must be won back to their rightful Lord, reinstated in the kingdom of life. For this Christ lived and died. As a king He came into the world to destroy the works of the devil, and win back man's allegiance to Himself. The whole ministry of Christ was built about this one central idea of a kingdom. "The Kingdom of Heaven is at hand." "Jesus came into Galilee preaching the gospel of the kingdom of God." "I must preach the kingdom of God to other cities also; for therefore am I sent." That wonderful Sermon on the Mount was a partial exposition of the law of this kingdom. He commissioned His disciples to "go preach, saying, the Kingdom of Heaven is at hand." To the "seventy," He said, "Say unto them, the Kingdom of God is come nigh unto you." And in all His earthly ministry He never let go His kingly prerogative Even in lowliest service, He was kingly. He was king in the presence of Pilate, in the midst of the mob, in His suffering on the cross, in His promise to the dying thief, in His triumphant resurrection, and in His regal ascension. He was a king in the splendor of His claims, in the grandeur of His promises, in the sublimity of His prophecies, in the righteousness of His judgments, in the equity of His laws, in the vastness of His realm, in the countless multitude of His subjects. For what other king were ever such weapons forged as truth and love? For what other sovereign have men displayed such exalted moral courage? For what other "leader and commander" have so many thousands died with quiet heart and forgiving word? What other king ever conquered by patient love and won victories by dying? What other king was ever anointed of God a "leader and commander" to all people? He was the very "King of kings." And the doctrine of a spiritual kingdom was the one theme of His teaching.

At this time when He is about to utter His first parable, when the enthusiasm is at the highest, and crowds were proclaiming Him king, we see a division work becoming apparent. While this work began at the very beginning of His ministry, yet so marked was it at the time of this parable that many immediately went back and walked no more with Him. The truth had at last entered their minds that His kingdom was spiritual, a kingdom of regenerate character.

He was gathering around Him a little band of true members of His kingdom, into whose minds He poured the wealth of His kingly teaching, which through them was to be scattered broadcast over the world. To this little inner circle, the first of the many that shall fill the earth, He spake directly, without any other veil to His deep meanings than the human words which conveyed them. These were loyal subjects, with hearts ready for the seed, with minds already subject to the laws of His spiritual kingdom, for Christ was a king in every life of this little army now being marshalled for the conquest of the world. Others might sit with His loyal disciples, but to them alone was He giving the invulnerable armor of His own graces, and the keen-edged sword of divine truth.

"*But to those without He spake in parables.*"

The disciples saw that He made a distinction between themselves and the multitude that crowded to hear His teachings, and they inquired of him the reason. Before giving them a direct reply, He lays down the principle on which His action is based. "Whosoever hath, to him shall be given, and he shall have more abundance, but whosoever hath not, from him shall be taken away even that he hath." Whoever possesses any truth, shows the ability to receive truth. Whoever does not possess, shows want of ability to receive. Whoever, by possession of the first truths of the kingdom, shows his fitness and ability to receive higher teachings, will receive abundance; but he who has not received the beginning, cannot receive the completion. The man who rejects the spirit of the kingdom, is unprepared to understand its laws.

Spiritual meanings are ever hidden from the hard-hearted and selfish, and revealed to those who are willing and able to receive them; while the highest truths are revealed to the true heart of faith, and always concealed from the careless and gross-hearted. That man whose heart possesses truth has a magnet within himself to which all truth is in some degree attracted. He has that in him which makes all that is true attractive to him, and with every new acquisition of truth there comes an increase of pleasure in its pursuit. When a man has a little information on any subject, every item concerning it is read with pleasure, and is naturally assimilated with the knowledge previously acquired. When the heart is not open to the dawning of the light, its later, noonday beams will only dazzle and blind.

But our Saviour had a further meaning. The soul that rejects His truth shall see going from him the very opportunity of hearing the plain, direct commands of Christ, and will hear them only in parables which he may interpret to his own condemnation.

Christ had spoken plainly to all alike of His mission as a king. Some received the truth, and thus were prepared for a higher education in divine things. Others had so misused and abused their ability to receive spiritual truth that it is only casting pearls before swine to preach the kingdom of heaven to them. Disuse or misuse of their higher faculties had left them unable to see any meaning beyond the physical. The years of His earthly ministry are few, and the causes of the world's reformation must all be put in motion. Shall He now continue to scatter seed on all alike? He does not, but takes the few who were fitted by the possession of the first principles of the kingdom for a more rapid growth in this higher knowledge, into a closer relation with Himself, that He might teach them more fully the mysteries of the kingdom of God. To them the Saviour will give more and more abundantly of His rich gifts. To the multitude who had rejected this plain proclamation of His mission, He will veil His meaning in parables.

"*They will not hear: therefore in judgment I speak to them in parables.*"

What is helpful truth to one is judgment to another. The Christian rejoices in the thought that there is a God who knoweth all things; while to the "wicked" the thought of Jehovah's omniscience is a terrible judgment. Christ had spoken tenderly and plainly to all concerning the beauties and glories of His kingdom. He had earnestly besought them to receive its sacred privileges and blessings. They had heard and rejected. They despised His truths when they saw that His kingdom was not of this world, and thus proved themselves unfit to be taken into that inner circle of truth-seekers who heard Him gladly. The higher truths and aspirations of the Christian life are always foolishness to one without the kingdom. The "Sermon on the Mount" would have been but pearls cast before swine to the crowd gathered at Sinai. Christ's truths were the revelation of Himself to the souls of men. Reject His teachings, and you reject His life. If, therefore, in judgment He withdraws Himself and His teachings from you, He is but acting according to your desire

Jesus had truths to state which were of great importance to His disciples in their ministry as his witnesses. To state these to the multitude would only excite them to greater hatred, and endanger the life and ministry of both Himself and His disciples. He, therefore, chose to state the doctrine so that if their hearts were right, if any capability to receive the truth were left in them, they would catch His meaning ; but if they were gross of heart, malignant, haters of the truth, they would not understand.

From this time forward the Saviour veils his truths from the multitude. He does not abandon them. He does not refuse to teach them. But they hear no more sermons of the mount, no more direct unfoldings of the rich truths of His kingdom.

Those within the kingdom are no longer servants, but nearest friends, to whom He reveals the highest meanings of His life, and inspires them with the promise of eternal life in His likeness. Those without the kingdom are aliens. To them, parables are as judgments. Having eyes, they see not the truth: having ears, they hear not the meaning of the words that come to them.

Yet Christ does not completely withdraw Himself when they reject His teachings. He still speaks to them in parables. There may be some who will hear aright. Some even of those who would have been aroused to dangerous anger by plain statement of the truth, by continual repetition of it in parables might be led up unsuspecting to a state of mind where truth could be received. "It is a blessing to have truth near, though separated by a veil." Moreover, this was the only chance left them to hear the word of life. They had rejected the plain statement of the truth, and this is the only method left by which it can possibly reach them. And these pictures from nature have a power of clinging to the mind in a way that sometimes effects what the most earnest direct teachings fail to accomplish.

Thus judgment and mercy, side by side, were sifting the multitude, and separating those within the kingdom from those without. By parables they may yet receive the truth; and if they still reject it, there is the palliation that the truth is veiled. Mercy and judgment may not be separated, but the latter will be held in abeyance until all the facts of the Saviour's life are acted out; until the cross, and the grave, and the empty tomb have fully established His kingdom and made its mysteries clear. Then after the Spirit has come, His trained disciples with clear vision, renewed hearts, and divine guidance, will preach this kingdom with marvelous power. The seed sown by the Saviour in these parables which still cling to the minds of the multitude, watered by the Spirit, now, under the earnest teaching of the disciples, may yet bring forth some harvest of ripened convictions. Who can tell how much of the harvest gathered at Pentecost grew from the earlier sowing of the Son of God?

"HEAR YE THE PARABLE OF THE SOWER."

"In the morning sow thy seed, and in the evening withhold not thine hand." Eccles. 11 : 6.

"In the name of God advancing,
  Sow thy seed at morning light ;
Cheerily the furrows turning,
  Labor on with all thy might.
Look not to the far-off future,
  Do the work which nearest lies ;
Sow thou must before thou reapest,
  Rest at last is labor's prize.

"Standing still is dangerous ever,
  Toil is meant for Christians now ;
Let there be, when evening cometh,
  Honest sweat on every brow ;
And the Master shall come smiling,
  At the setting of the sun,
Saying, as He pays thy wages,
  'Good and faithful one, well done !'"

From unknown German Author.

"HEAR YE THE PARABLE OF THE SOWER."

Matt. 13, *Mark* 4, *Luke* 8.

Christ challenges the closest attention to this first parable.

Let us give heed to the Master's words, asking, as sincere disciples, for the interpretation, while we examine the parable and its exposition by our Lord.

It is a part of that great revelation of Himself which God has made to His people. Jehovah is become the seed of a divine life within man, and the husbandman to cultivate that life to a perfect harvest. The King of kings is become the Father of His people; the omnipotent God reveals Himself as the tenderly merciful and long-suffering Redeemer; the Judge of all the earth bows in deep humiliation to bear His people's burdens; the omniscient One, with His own blood, blots out of His sight the sins of His redeemed. We cannot of ourselves add anything to the sum of holiness, and even as we try to reflect the holiness of God, it is marred by our shadows, and the mirrored image is often a deformed one. With our reflection of the gentleness, charity, and zeal of Christ, we are ever mingling our own harshness and coldly formal service. We are sinful, and, strive as we may, we always fall short of any great attainment in righteousness. Yet the seed of a divinely perfect life is sown within us, and the infinitely wise Sower, who knew the end from the beginning, has prophesied a full harvest. This seed is the "word of the kingdom." "Thy word is truth,"—the truth that scattered in human hearts brings "the kingdom of God and His righteousness" into the world of human life and sinfulness.

This parable, so wonderfully fitted to the occasion when the divine Teacher used it to describe that crowd standing by Genesareth, is as accurately true to-day in every assembly to which the gospel is preached. Four classes of hearers were defined then, and all four are here to-day. You belong to one, and only one, of these classes.

THE SCENE.

What a picture is here suggested by the inspired writer! A great multitude full of enthusiasm, curious, excited, crowding out of Capernaum and the neighboring villages, eager to catch every word of the wonderful Teacher. Pressed by the throng, this Teacher steps into a boat, and a few strokes of the oars carry Him and His disciples away from the crowd, yet He waits near enongh to the shore for all the multitude to hear. Only a narrow strip of water separated His body from the crowd, but what an infinite distance separated Him in spirit from them! A rude pulpit, that unsteady fishing boat, but from it came a message as abiding and as powerful as truth from God.

Five hundred feet below the level of the sea, in a cleft of the hills, lies the lake of Galilee. Thus, as if from the lowest station He could reach, Christ spake to the multitude crowding the shore that sloped gently up from the water's edge to the mountain ridge above. Before His eyes were large and busy towns and hamlets, and terraced hills covered with fruitful vineyards,—Gennesaret, the "garden of princes."

Probably as His eyes return from the Father's face, He sees a sower scattering grain on the hill-side above and behind the waiting crowd that stood like the ploughed field ready to receive the seed. We can almost see them turn to look as He bids them,

"*Behold, the sower went forth to sow.*"

Galilee's lake still lies among her silent hills, pure and clear as when this parable was spoken; but sail and oar now seldom disturb her waters. The villages and vineyards that once lay all along her shores are to be traced only in a few ruins; and the crowds that listened to the voice of Jesus are two thousand years away beyond death. Still that voice speaks to us, and still those seeds of truth fall like heavenly manna upon our hungry souls, and to-day are producing a richer and grander harvest in our world than even when they came in all their freshness and vigor from the Master's heart. Rather, we are still reaping the fruits of that sowing of the divine husbandman. These fruits are in all our thoughts and hopes, in all our homes and cities, fruits that have their root in that Master's life and work two thousand years ago.

THE SEED.

"Seeing ye have purified your souls in your obedience to the truth unto unfeigned love of the brethren, love one another from the (clean) heart fervently; having been begotten again, not of corruptible seed, but of incorruptible, through the word of God, which liveth and abideth." I Peter 1: 23.

" The seed is the word of God."

All teachings are seeds that must produce some fruit in every life into which they fall. All uttered thoughts are seeds that hold within themselves some life for future growth. In what a high sense must this be true of the "Word of God," which He spake who was Himself the power within all His teachings!

Observe this seed. It is from God, who knows man thoroughly, his history, his needs, and his capabilities; who also knows the truth in its own greatness, in its fitness to deliver man into highest freedom, and in its life-giving power as represented to the world in Jesus. The all-wise God, knowing the end from the beginning, has given this seed of life as perfectly adapted to supply man's need, and to grow up in him to an endless life.

Christ scatters the seed with a perfect knowledge of all this, and with an eternal purpose that it shall produce an abundant harvest in every good and honest heart. For us the Bible, like a treasure house, contains this seed. "Search the scriptures, for in them ye think ye have eternal life, and these are they which bear witness of me." Treat this book reverently then, for it holds the words of life, the truth concerning Him who is "the way, the truth, and the life," to every good and honest heart.

Christ is both seed and Sower. "*He that soweth the good seed is the Son of man.*" Matt. 13:37. But He is also the Word of truth, the holy *Logos*, the perfect expression of the thought of God.

"God having of old time spoken unto the fathers in the prophets by divers portions and in divers manners, hath at the end of these days spoken unto us in His Son."

God hath been made manifest unto us who do believe in Him. Prophets told us the truth of God; the Son revealed the person of God. They knowing only in part, could reveal only in part; He knowing the truth in the very counsels of the Father in all its fullness, uttered truth in all its greatness and wealth. Coming through human prophets and teachers by human language and symbols, it came slowly by changing modes and with varying meaning. Coming by a Son, yea in a Son, who bore in His own nature the express image of the Father, the manifestation of the truth was perfect, complete and unchangeable.

The great and wide universe, with its unnumbered worlds, with all its infinite variety and wealth of life and beauty, is but the incarnation of a few of the thoughts of God. All the tremendous energy manifested in the movements of the worlds of the universe, and all the accuracy displayed in their perfect order, are simply partial expressions of the energy and accuracy of the divine Mind. They ought to be, and are becoming more and more, the illustrations of the workings of that Being whose nature is truth. They are the utterances of the mind of God, in a language we only partially understand, and at the best we can read from them a very indefinite knowledge of Jehovah. We would see, and God would have us see, a grander and nearer, a richer and plainer, expression of Himself. We needed an expression of our God that could come to our seared consciences with the voice of life's Omniscient Judge, that could speak to our sin-narrowed souls with the expanding, exalting voice of eternal life, that could speak to our darkened hearts with the voice of the Father of lights, that could meet our repentance with divine forgiveness, that could heal human sorrow with the compassion of a holy comforter, that could quicken hope by a revelation of the unseen glories of God and Heaven. God speaking in His Son is such an expression. Christ speaks God's will, but it is by speaking God's nature. He is the express image of the Father, the very utterance of His Being to our needy human race.

This living Christ is the power within the seed, the Word within the word, that breaks the husk and brings forth a new life and growth within the soul. This divine life within the uttered word of truth, when it falls into proper soil, will put forth energy in a new life that shall strike its roots ever deeper and deeper, and send the foliage and blossoms and fruits higher and higher in growth towards Him who sowed the seed. The fault of failure to produce a good harvest cannot be in the sower or the seed. Indeed, if you scatter good seed in any manner upon soil properly prepared, it will grow. If failure come with good seed, the trouble is in the soil or its preparation. The Master illustrates this clearly and forcibly in the four classes of hearers.

FIRST CLASS OF HEARERS.

"And when he sowed, some fell by the wayside, and the fowls came and devoured them up." (Heb. 2:1; Acts 26:28; Matt. 22:5; Isa. 53:1.)

Christ's disciples were too familiar with the scene immediately around them to have any difficulty in understanding the letter of the parable, but they seek to know its deeper meaning. And the words, *"who hath ears to hear, let him hear,"* with which He closed the parable, must have challenged the attention of the most thoughtless, while it was a direct summons to all in that crowd who understood Him, to look for a meaning deeper and richer than the mere picture with which they were all familiar. The letter of the parable is easily understood, but what is the spiritual truth it holds for us?

As we study this "word of the kingdom," let us try to catch its full meaning, and by applying its lessons to our own lives, give the "seed" fullest opportunity to grow even to an hundred fold in good and honest hearts.

The whole field was sown, but in Palestine, as in the far west of our own land, there are few fences, and the feet of many travelers have worn a hard path across the ploughed and harrowed surface. The Master's explanation of this part of the parable is, "*When anyone heareth the word of the kingdom, and understandeth it not, then cometh the wicked one, and catcheth away that which was sown in the heart.*"

We cannot justly make our ignorance a reason for not believing, yet if we cannot easily understand the teachings of Christ we are very apt to feel ourselves under no obligation to give them any further attention. Nor have we any right to make the obscurity of the word and the difficulty of our surroundings the excuses for our continued neglect of duty. Christ shows here the fallacy of all such pleas by the expression which in the text is translated "understandeth it not." Literally, it is "ináttention," neglecting to bring together in the mind for careful consideration the truths we hear. No one can be blamed for not understanding a subject which by actual, careful investigation he has proved to be beyond his capacity; but he is deserving of censure if he fails to understand a matter which is vital to him simply because he will not bring his mind to attend to it.

"*Then*," and not till then, "*cometh the wicked one*," "Satan," St. Luke says, "*and catcheth away that which was sown in the heart.*" Originally the soil was all alike. The whole field was well ploughed and harrowed, and the soil of the path is now as fertile as any other part of the field.

A fertile heart may become like a hard path under a long procession of evil thoughts, ungodly wishes and sinful deeds. Satan cannot steal away seed that is covered in the heart, and it is our fault if the ground is so hard that the seed can find no place to take root. It is our fault that we give no attention, that we do not carefully examine the truths of life, but without thought push them aside. It is our fault that, while hearing with the ear, we give no attention with the heart. Satan catches away only that which is left exposed upon the surface.

If Christ be true, these teachings of His are of infinite worth, affecting our life here, and our fate for all eternity. Is it the part of wisdom, of even ordinary good sense, to push them aside without careful examination? Yet many have no other reason than ignorance for their rejection of Christ. Rejecting the deepest truths and noblest gifts of life without any personal examination as to the validity of testimony or credibility of witnesses.

What a picture this is of many hearers in all our churches! They come with the multitude to keep holy-day, but the seed falls upon inattentive hearts, as rain falls upon the paved street. Their church-going is often a sort of weekly opiate, with which to quiet the conscience, or a mask to deceive the world, and sometimes themselves, and yet with an unexpressed hope that God will count their church-going as a favorable item in their final account.

St. Luke (12:13) tells of such a hearer. Christ had been preaching to the people an earnest sermon against all forms of hypocrisy, and showing them the great value of a soul, at the same time promising the Holy Spirit to help them in all trials and sufferings while preaching the truth. "And one of the company said unto him, Master, speak to my brother that he divide the inheritance with me." Evidently the man had given no real attention to the sermon, and he deserved the severe rebuke he received. So it was with Agrippa, when Paul sowed the truth so faithfully, the seed bounded off from a hard and careless heart.

Occasionally we hear people say they have no aptitude for religion. What will such people do in heaven, where everything is religion? Others say they have no interest in "church-work," in other words, they do not have any interest in the work which the church has undertaken at the command of Christ. Will such people have any place in heaven, where the whole life is a special service under the command of Christ? These people, and they are many, are simply hardening the soil, and allowing the seed to die without fruit. Yet the Master has said, "Herein is my Father glorified, that ye bear much fruit, so shall ye be my disciples."

Sometimes the very habits of what is called our religious life become a mere "crust of formality," hard paths across the heart. Attendance upon the ordinances of the church ought to lead us nearer to God, yet how often while the body is obedient to the form of worship the mind is far away. This half-listening, this not attending to the word, is fatal to any true reception of the truth, and only increases the difficulty in the way of growth. More and more becoming incapable of true repentance, such people have neither care nor fear. Their condition does not disturb them, for sin has no deep meaning to them. They know in a general way that they ought to prepare to meet their God, but their hearts are not stirred with the thought of that great certainty, and they are apt soon to grow indifferent to all things spiritual.

A man gets into this hardened condition, so that the Gospel message has no helpful meaning to him, only because he has exposed his heart as a common road to evil influences. He listens to the gospel without objection, it may be, but it arouses no personal interest, for it has fallen on a hardened surface. However he may apply it to others, to himself it is only a social or intellectual culture, or a listening out of curiosity, or for appearance sake. The Bible does not take hold of his thoughts as his ledger does. Sin and righteousness are not nearly so vital to him as the daily stock report, the condition of his bank, the prospect of harvest, or his physical health or comfort. The good soil may be there, but it is hard. While gracious influences rain upon it, they run off as from a hardened path, and the first hour's march of the old intruders will make it as hard and barren as ever. The truth may be scattered by loving hands thickly upon it, but winged day-dreams and wicked thoughts steal many a holy seed, and the heavy tread of evil passions and sinful habits soon crushes the others to their death.

The farmer does not blame the birds of the air for following the instincts of their nature in stealing his grain so much as he does the trespassers who have worn the path across his rich and well-ploughed fields. Too often the soil in which the word of God should have been received, and where it would have taken root, is allowed to become the highway of the soul's greatest enemies. To such a hearer the command is: submit yourself to the deep ploughing of the Spirit and the law, and when the heart is thus broken up, scatter in it the seeds of truth. For if the Holy Spirit has deeply furrowed the heart, we know that the divine Sower has scattered there seeds of vast spiritual endowments, and He who sowed the seed gives the sunshine and the rain, the dew and the shade of night, all in proper measure for a full and perfect harvest. But it is ours to keep away all evil birds, and to see that the soil is not tramped so hard that the seed can find no place to grow.

This first part of the parable ought to touch keenly every hearer of the word. Is your heart's soil thoroughly prepared to receive the falling seed, or is there across it a well tramped path of inattention, careless listening, irreverence, any evil habit of mind or body? Remember, there is one watching to steal away the seed that falls upon any spot that is not prepared for its reception. When you hear and yet neglect the word, you practically throw it to Satan. When we think of this, and remember how little of the word we carry away from God's house and from our daily study of His book, is it any wonder that so many who hear the life-giving word bring forth no fruit?

Do not blame surrounding circumstances, household cares, and strong temptations, for stealing away the seed; but put the truth so deeply into your life that none will be left upon the surface for these hungry birds to feed upon.

We all constantly experience a fading of good impressions because we leave them upon a hardened surface where they cannot grow, instead of covering them with prayer, and cultivating them by an active pursuit of the duties they inculcate. To seize and use every good thing, whether it be impression, thought, or opportunity to bless others, is the only sure way of getting for ourselves its harvest of blessing. Sometimes amid the darkness of a midnight storm, the vivid lightning gives an instant view of all the surrounding landscape, and shows the path from which we have wandered. So there occasionally flashes across the mind a vivid view of truth that quickens faith, awakens high aspirations, rouses the will to overthrow some habit of sin, stimulates to renewed consecration of life, and shows the path of duty. Why does this so quickly vanish? Because we give it no hearty invitation to remain, no home to live in, no duty to perform. We receive it without attention. And yet it is possible for us so to receive these occasional flashes of good as to have them increase to a frequency that will make our whole life a bright day of light and blessing.

Strong graces, like strong powers of mind and body, require constant exercise. Inaction is certain death to them. As intellectual idleness means mental famine, so idle Christian is synonymous with dying Christian. All graces have their infancy, a seed time, when life is just beginning, and their way to full growth and fruitfulness is through exercise and constant watchfulness.

Yet how many are never strong Christians because they are ever waiting and wishing for strong graces, instead of cultivating what they have to their fullest growth and greatest strength. Every true Christian has within him the growing seed of a perfect life. If the full harvest does not come, it is not the fault of the perfect seed or the divine Sower. How many turn from the sanctuary every Sabbath day without profit from the service, because they hear without attention. They receive an impression which they know should be immediately put into practice, yet it is neglected until even the memory of it is gone. There are others so thoroughly selfish and vain as to have no spot in the heart where seed can grow. It falls upon them as upon others, but bounds off as from a hard sidewalk. If they ever forget themselves long enough to think of the truth, it is to blame the birds for stealing away the seed. They forget that if Satan had not taken away the truth from them, the incessant tramp of their own vain conceits and selfish gratifications would soon have crushed it to death.

Too many people live with the heart unfenced. It is a public common, standing open with loud invitation to all travelers to walk across, or even camp within. It has no sacred place, no holy of holies, where only the great High Priest may enter. Instead of jealously guarding every impression, the life is left open to all the vile seeds that float in the social atmosphere. Seeds whose fruits are envy, anger, suspicion, sensuality, and all manner of uncharitableness. Thus, instead of carefully loosening the soil whenever it has become hardened by the long-continued tramp of a bad habit, they allow seed to fall upon a surface entirely unprepared, only to die or be stolen by the enemy.

How often we should be ashamed and self-condemned if we could gather up the truths we have lost by inattention, and see them in their origin, their present meaning, the fruits they would have produced, their influence upon all our future life, their fitness to prepare us for the reception of other truths, and then contrast them with the things to which we did give our attention. Truth driven away by some selfish thought. God-given beauty refused for ashes of earth. A growing seed of priceless worth rejected for seed of thorns and weeds.

It may be that some good seeds have fallen on your heart in childhood before the hard path was worn, that would spring towards the sun if you would but break the hard crust that covers them.

A visitor to a prison saw there a woman charged with the murder of her child. Every effort was made to arouse her to a sense of her guilt, but nothing pierced her hardness. The visitor was frequently at the prison, and his ministry was received by all save this one. Passing one day by a nursery, he saw in the hot-house some common garden flowers. He knew that the childhood of this woman had been passed in the country, and trusted that her girl nature had known a love for

"SOME FELL BY THE WAYSIDE." 63

flowers. He purchased a bouquet and took it to the prison. Going into the cell, he placed the flowers and a copy of the gospel of St. John on the little iron table, and went out into the hall where he could see and not be seen. The prisoner soon came to examine what had been given her. Through the grated door the visitor saw her look at the book and drop it on the floor. The flowers she touched and smelled. Memory began to do its work, and her face was soon buried among the flowers. The tears came, and there upon her knees, with her head and hands upon the table, she went back again to her innocent childhood in her country home. The snow and cold outside were changed to summer sunshine. The hard, sin-burnt heart was aglow with love for the mother watching from the home window. The little fingers were busy plucking flowers in the old home garden. The hard crust was broken, and the seeds that fell on the child's heart so long ago are now blossoming and bearing fruit in the reformed, regenerated woman's life. Many a one whom we call hardened might become a fruitful Christian if once the crust were broken. The Spirit can plough, and loving hands can sow the seed. Let the seed be ever falling, for we know not when the Spirit is at work in another's heart, and some seed may find a loosened, fertile spot in which to grow.

SECOND CLASS OF HEARERS.

"The Lord is nigh unto them that are of a broken heart, and saveth such as be of a contrite spirit." *Ps.* 34: 18.

"We have the heavenly assurance that the path of the just is to shine more and more unto the perfect day. But this blessed truth involves its opposite, that the path of the wicked must grow darker and darker unto the total night, ... unless he give heed to the voice which calls him out of this darkness, and turn to the light which is ever striving to illumine it."

Guesses at Truth.

SECOND CLASS OF HEARERS.

"*Some fell upon stony places, where they had not much earth; and forthwith they sprang up, because they had no deepness of earth; and when the sun was up, they were scorched, and because they had no root they withered away.*" St. Matt. 13: 5, 6.

"*They on the rock are they, which, when they hear, receive the word with joy; and these have no root, which for a time believe, and in time of temptation fall away.*" St. Luke 8: 13.

By a comparison between St. Matthew and St. Luke we discover what is meant by "stony places" and "rock." Not a spot in the field where stones lie thickly upon the surface, but where a large rock lies beneath a shallow covering of earth.

The field appeared to be all alike until the path was worn. Rocks could not be seen. The seed is scattered over the whole field and, save upon the path, takes root and grows. The summer sun gets higher in the heavens every day, and sends his hot rays down upon the grain. The path is bare and hard, but elsewhere over all the field the grain has taken root and is growing vigorously. What a prospect for the Autumn! The soil is fertile. It contains every element necessary to produce a full and abundant harvest. Lying about the roots of the grain are stores of life to paint the leaves, strengthen the stalk, and fill its treasury with golden grain. The sun in the heavens pumps these elements of life from the earth through the roots to every part of leaf and stalk. The higher the plant grows, the higher into the heavens the sun climbs, that he may send increasing force to do this all-important work of developing the whole life of the field to its utmost capability. But as the weeks go by we notice here and there a fading of the rich hue of health. The green turns to yellow. The leaves curl downwards as if striving to avoid the gaze of the sun, and in a little while these spots are dead. Why? The grain grew, sending roots downward and stalks upward. The roots collected the life from the soil, and the sun pumped that life up through the plant. After a time the roots had drawn all the life out of the soil, and were creeping along the hard surface of the rock, vainly striving by every crevice to get through to the moist earth below. Inexorably the sun kept on at his work. His office was not the preparation of the soil, but the drawing from the soil of nourishment for the plant that must bear the grain. The roots are doing their best to supply all that the growing life of the plant calls for, but they cannot feed on the rock. The sun keeps on pumping from plant to fruit, from roots to plant. So the roots must now surrender their life to feed the plant. Nor does the sun stop there. Higher and higher he climbs. He has the same work to do for all the myriad forms of earthly life. If he should stop, they would die. Hence, when the life is all drawn out of the soil, the roots must give up their life, and then the plant itself must give forth its strength and die.

How close the analogy between this law of plant life and the law of human life? Whatever is superficial is apt to be transitory. Shallowness quickly puts forth all its energy and dies. Not having much root, it exhibits all its growth and strength upon the surface. Those who have little knowledge are usually forward and noisy; they have little of the joy of the true student, whose greatest pleasure is in the silent companionship with knowledge, the deeply-rooted life that cannot be seen by others. How little of the deep and abiding joy of a symmetrical Christian does that soul know whose life is in what he does and says before the world, more than in what he is before God.

There seems to be an improvement, however, in the condition of this class over the first class. There is here some life. In the first class, the seed did not even take root. Here it takes root, grows quickly, as with special fertility of soil, and promises a large harvest. But we soon discover that this improvement is but specious, and that the rapid growth upward is from lack of room to grow downward. There it was hardened soil above, here it is rock below. That had been made hard lately, and is upon the surface where you may see it; this is far enough below to deceive you. Yet there is a real advance, for there the seed had no life; here it has been received and is growing. You may break up the path only to find a rock beneath and the seed all blown away or stolen, and the Spirit can break up the stony heart as easily as the hard one.

Failure in life is not among wayside hearers only; but many who hear "gladly," fail to bring forth the real harvest of life, yea, fail to live until harvest time comes. They are inconsiderate and impulsive, as the members of the preceding class were inattentive and careless. The "joy of the Holy Ghost" is unknown to them because they have "no root in themselves." There may be here and there a stalk that is able to get a single root over the edge of the rock, and thus live a sickly life even to the time of ingathering; but its harvest is puny, the grains are all shriveled through lack of life's vigor, and when at last it falls before the reaper, no golden seeds roll out into the earth to grow to another harvest.

Our Saviour interprets the meaning of this class as "*he that heareth the word and anon with joy receiveth it, yet hath he not root in himself, but dureth for awhile; for when tribulation or persecution ariseth because of the word, by and by he is offended.*"

The seed here is the same as in the former case, the "word of the kingdom." Those upon whom it falls are attentive; they are interested; they receive the seed and cover it into their hearts, where it takes root and grows rapidly. In times of special interest, when many are receiving the word and accepting it openly, this part of the parable is apt to be too frequently illustrated. Excitable natures are easily stirred, and receive the seed without due preparation of heart. They accept the gospel with joy, and go forth valiantly, but they have not counted the cost. The warfare is a long one, with an enemy rich in resources and of skill unequalled. Their earnestness is volatile, quickly noticed, and soon loses its strength. They are seeking their own happiness rather than a change of character. They run swiftly while the street is smoothly paved and many are near to applaud; but "by and by" the way is rough, the special interest is over, and the crowds have gone to other excitements.

Tribulation and persecution, which ought to strengthen Christian character, prove to this class a stumbling block over which they fall. They have put on the robes of disciples and easily use their speech, but in character there is no change. The old heart is still there under a new covering.

They receive the word with joy, but their joy is thoughtless, a stirring of the emotions, not the peace of a changed nature. Their heart has been touched only upon the surface, not smitten with that blow of Jehovah that makes a stream of living water flow as from the cleft rock, full of life-giving power to the end of life's journey.

For a time they "did run well," but after awhile they are missed occasionally from the prayer-meeting, they are less active in the Sunday School. For a time they rejoiced to be able to testify to the world that they were Christ's. After the time of special interest, when persecution arose because of the word, the sneer and laugh blowing like a hot, withering wind upon them, they drooped and died. For a while Sabbaths were sacred times, and the services of God's house a pleasure and a profit. But temptation came, and the time of worship was neglected more and more for the opportunity it gave to attend to some little matter forgotten during the week. Soon the duties of the week that with a little stretch of conscience might be called not sinful, are postponed until the leisure of Sunday. Other desecrations of God's chosen holy day follow, and the surface religion is soon rubbed off. Thus the soul is once more put under obligation to sin. Such Christian character is shallow. The roots have come to the rock, and the soil is nearly all exhausted of life. Yet they are the people who are the quickest to resent any hint that they are in danger. They are only not narrow-minded; they are liberal. They are not narrow Christians, only shallow ones. They will soon be as bare of all Christian beauty and fruitfulness as the withered spot in yonder field of grain.

"By and by they are offended." Yes, they are easily offended. While the sense of the parable is "by and by they sin," yet in a commoner sense they are offended. They complain more than any other class within the church. The church is not managed properly, the singing does not suit them, the preacher is too pointed, the ushers are too slow, they do not believe in missions. They are offended because some of the Bible doctrines stand unchangeably before them with stern judgment upon their lives. All these complaints are mere excuses for their own superficial lives. Their religion is a matter of feeling, not of character. Feeling is transient; character is permanent. When that which aroused the feeling is gone, it subsides until moved by some new influence. Such religion is to true discipleship what a review, or a formal salute, is to a battle. Such hearing of the truth is playing with a divine gift, a mere wasting of heavenly, life-giving seed.

The members of this class are guided more by the judgments of others than by their own consciences. Their religion is a possession, not a being. They have "got religion" more than they have become religious. Having no root of life in themselves, but only in their surroundings, they are necessarily temporary Christians, so that when a change comes in their surrounding circumstances it changes their whole life.

Not only do excitable ones belong to this class who receive the seed and so quickly let it die, but many a calm and quiet one, listening thoughtfully Sunday after Sunday to divine truth, receives it only so far as to produce a fair external life. There is no change of heart. His character remains the same. In one class of these shallow hearers, feeling is the only soil into which the seed is received; while in this class, the intellect is all that is converted. One is heat without light, the heart's feelings running swiftly in a new road without the guidance of the head; the other is the head-light pointing in the right direction and lighting the way, but not advancing. In both there is soil enough to receive the seed, but not enough to sustain the full and continued growth. Under strong temptation they will fall away.

Even then the one will strive to retain

his pleasure in christian things, and the other will try to hold on to his outward christian life long after the roots are dead. Satan stole the seed of life from the wayside hearer without any trouble, but in this class he has to make some effort to destroy it. He witnesses the rapid growth, and tests it to see whether it be deeply rooted. He sends temptations, doubts, and causes of offense. The heat increases. A parley is held with the tempter. The soul sins, and christian character begins to wither. The more intensely the sun pours his heat upon a plant deeply rooted in good soil, the more rapid and fruitful the growth. The tropics receive the most direct rays of the sun, but are ever the richest in flower and fruit. Temptations are blessings if you endure them, and the true Christian is always strengthened by conflict. Even when he falls before any particular temptation he is humbled, and thus lifted up. (I Kings 21: 29; I Peter 5: 6; Jas. 4: 10.) When successfully resisted, temptations and persecutions strengthen and develop the christian life by compelling it to strike its roots ever deeper and deeper into the soil.

If the whole heart be changed, and thoroughly prepared for the growth of christian character, the hot sun of opposition will only compel it to grow more rapidly. But if the roots have but little soil, and the heart's centre be a rock, the growth will be rapid enough, but death will come to one after another of the fruits till all are dead before ripened. The same persecution that sent the true Christians to the stake, sent the shallow ones to reinforce the enemies of Christ.

Many a man who has been a pronounced Christian and is now as avowed in his infidelity, is an illustration of this part of the parable. He boldly affirms that he has tried Christianity, was sincere in his practice of it, and it is a failure. If he would study his case more closely and logically, he would see that he is proclaiming his own shallowness. He failed to prepare the soil properly for the new seed of life, and the rock beneath the surface prevented the permanent growth of a christian character. The rapid growth of so divine a plant soon exhausted all the real strength of so shallow a soil, and naught was left it but to die. The seed was God-given and perfect. He, not the seed, was the failure.

There are many who come to Christ as the young man who had kept all the commandments from his youth, but had in his heart a solid rock of avarice which he would not break up even for eternal life.

The "rock" of selfishness which is in nearly every human heart is a great obstacle to the growth of Christ's kingdom. You offer all to Christ. Do you mean it? Has the Spirit thoroughly ploughed your heart? Not merely made tender your feelings, and won the consent of your mind; but has he thoroughly sub-soiled your heart, so that there is no rock left? Are you ready to let your christian character grow everywhere, even if its roots crush out every pet sin and doubtful pleasure?

Foolish vanity stands like a great stone at the door of many hearts, otherwise good and honest. They are proud of what they appear to be; they boast of what they can do. If the seed takes root in them, it quickly strikes the rock of self, and then through lack of soil their religious life dies. The sun does not kill the plant. It dies only because the roots cannot find nourishment. Temptation and persecution and tribulation do not kill the christian life; they are only the occasion, not the cause of death. Death comes to a christian life only because there is no soil for its roots, no food for its sustenance—it is starved to death.

Notice that the members of this class are all professing Christians, either in the church or out of it. The first class did not even start. This class started joyfully, ran well during the time of excitement, then withdrew and died. Their weakness was radical—a root weakness. The heart, the very core of life, instead of being full of divine seed, was entirely hard. The old selfishness had never been properly ploughed up, hence their sorrow for sin was more a matter of pride than of repentance. They were sorry for the evil of their lives because of the unpleasant consequences they feared, and their humility was a temporary subjugation of the feelings, not a heart's lowly sense of unworthiness. The great mistake of multitudes within the church, and a larger number of judges without it, lies in their considering Christianity a mere matter of sentiment or feeling. The plain teaching of every part of this parable, the unmistakable declaration of Christ, is that the christian life comes from a divine birth within the soul, which must transform, by gradual but complete renewal, the whole nature of a man. It is not a possession, or an opinion, or even a belief, but a living, growing character.

THIRD CLASS OF HEARERS.

"Thou shalt love the Lord thy God with *all thy heart* and with all thy soul, and with all thy mind. This is the first and greatest commandment." *Matt.* 22: 37.

> "Full seldom doth a man repent, or use
>   Both grace and will to pick the vicious quitch
> Of blood and custom wholly out of him,
>   And make it clean, and plant himself afresh."
> *Tennyson.*

"All virtue and goodness tend to make men powerful in this world; but they who aim at the power have not the virtue. Again, virtue is its own reward, and brings with it the truest and highest pleasures; but they who cultivate it for the pleasure-sake are selfish, not religious, and will never have the pleasure, because they never can have the virtue."
J. H. Newman.

THIRD CLASS OF HEARERS.

"And some fell among thorns, and the thorns sprung up and choked them."

Here, again, the seed is the same as that which has been scattered upon the path and upon the stony places. This is a part of the same field, but the soil is not tramped, and no rocks are there. Yet when the good grain comes up, noxious weeds are growing as thickly as the grain.

The soil was fertile, and the ploughing had been deep and thorough, but the old roots had not been removed, hence they grew up rapidly with the good seed and choked it They drew the strength from the soil, and shaded the good grain from the sun.

In the first case the seed did not have any life in the soil. In the second it grew for a short time, then died. Here it retains the name to live, but brings no fruit to perfection. The seed is received into rich soil, is covered, and puts forth a good growth, and finding no rocks, it roots deeply. Yet, after a few weeks, if you will walk along the hardened path from which the grain has all been stolen, you will see occasional barren spots, with only the dead stalks remaining to mark the rocky place; and here and there, also, you will notice large patches of grain mingled with thorns, cockle, mustard, or whatever may be the besetting thorn, or weed, of that particular region.

The hearer of this class is not stupid, nor hardened as in the first class, nor one of mere feeling, as in the second class. In the first, there was no growing life. In the second, growth near the surface (both above and below), no high-reaching fruits above, because there was no deeply-rooted life below. In the third we find the roots striking deeply into fertile soil and a rapid growth upward, but thorns are growing thickly with the grain The birds could not steal the seed, for it was received into the soil and covered. The sun could not wither it, for the roots found no rock. Why, then, has no fruit come to perfection? The word has fallen upon lives thoroughly ploughed, no rocks are there, and no paths are yet worn across the heart. They keep the word through all trials and difficulties, but they keep it with an increasing growth of weeds. When the heart was broken up, the old thorn-roots were not killed, and now they are growing more rapidly than the good grain.

It is another illustration of a heart trying to serve both God and mammon, trying to be both religious and worldly, with the hope of getting the best out of both, and thus failing to get the good out of either. The heart's powers are summoned in so many directions, and spread over so many conflicting interests, that there is not strength in any one spot to bring fruit to perfection.

The capability of every soil is fixed. It can furnish just so much food for the life growing from it. If all that life be of good seed, and the soil be properly prepared, an abundant harvest will be produced. Every weed or thorn requires food for its growth, and takes away just that much of nourishment from the good grain. Every life is capable, with proper preparation, of bringing forth an abundant harvest of good and holy fruits. But if bad seed gets in and mingles its growth with that which is good, all the good and true will be weakened, and much care is needed that it be not entirely destroyed. Many a man struggles through all his adult life to get rid of thorns whose seed was sown in his childhood. It is not enough simply to prevent evil seeds falling within your own or your child's life. The field that is carefully fenced and unceasingly guarded will yet grow full of the rankest weeds and thorns, unless thoroughly cultivated and sown with good seed. If good seed is not sown with careful, continued cultivation in every young heart, evil will soon be seen there in vigorous growth. The fate of the seed depends upon the condition of the soil. If properly prepared, all evil seeds and roots removed, and only good seed allowed to grow, an abundant harvest of fullest value will be gathered.

The Master's interpretation of this verse is: "*He also that received seed among the thorns, is he that heareth the word; and the care of this world and the deceitfulness of riches choke the word, and he becometh unfruitful.*"

St. Luke says, 8: 14: "*And that which fell among thorns are they, which, when they have heard, go forth, and are choked with cares and pleasures of this life, and bring no fruit to perfection.*"

"*Are choked.*" As if smothered by the deadly gases that deepen sleep and stop the life. Gradually these evil weeds crowd out the good seed, robbing it of air and light. Evil never succeeds in conquering life by a sudden assault, but always gradually, and usually without being noticed. First dulling the senses, then smothering the life.

The cares and riches and pleasures of

this life, in contrast with care for heavenly things; striving for worldly success as contrasted with striving for eternal life. The cares that threaten, and those that flatter; the poverty that oppresses, and the riches that unduly elate. The two extremes are touched in order to cover all the wide interval between them.

This bringing of the seed of truth to a perfect harvest is everyone's business, and the rich are no more exempt from its duties and dangers than the poor. The poor man's toil and fear of days when work cannot be found; the struggle against poverty, or the appearance of need; the wife's unremitting household cares, and anxious fears for children growing daily into greater dangers; the unrelaxing, burdensome effort to give the appearance of greater wealth, are as dangerously deceitful as the rich man's care and anxiety. Yet the hard pressure of poverty is not more dangerous to spiritual life than the flattery of heartless parasites, or the false trust the rich man is ever tempted to put in the power of his wealth, or the luxuries and pleasures which riches too often pour in upon the soul to enfeeble and destroy it. These and other cares of this life weaken and choke the growth of the Christ-life in many a fertile heart. They exhaust the heart's best affections and overshadow the good seed with a rank, poisonous growth. They are robbers, for there are robbers everywhere on earth, and the bad will steal from the good, and might will trample down right wherever opportunity is found.

The commonest tramp of an evil care, or passion, or pleasure, is often permitted to get into the most secret chambers of our lives to steal away our most sacred treasures, and murder our most holy affections. And how easily and continually do we allow all manner of trifling annoyances and anxieties to commit petty larceny on our christian graces. The commonest household cares are sometimes allowed so to engross us that the good seed is crowded out of our lives. Every species of thorn-roots, all forms of inordinate love of things good in themselves, every wrong use of even right things, every variety of intemperance, all are ready with open hand to choke the life out of the good seed in our hearts.

All these things, cares, riches and pleasures, are entirely innocent in themselves, but they become enemies of all true life when they take the place of better things. We all have "cares of this life," and it would be a sad thing for our best life if we were without them; but is there no danger of having our life so absorbed in these cares that we have no room for anything better? When your work is greater than yourself, you are doomed. "What great things he has accomplished!" Wonders of achievement! But what of himself? Is his whole life expressed in these works? They will soon die. Has any man a right so to absorb himself in the cares of this life as to have no time for discharging his special obligations to God?

"DECEITFULNESS OF RICHES."

Wealth wields in all human society an enormous power for good or evil. Under the control of a lowly Christian heart, riches may be a blessing of rarest quality; but under the guidance of selfish ambition, they are sure to prove a curse even to their possessor. In itself wealth is a blessing to be received with deep thankfulness, for in its proper use God is glorified and the world made better; the deceitfulness of riches is a curse to rich and poor alike. The poor man may be as miserly with his penny as the rich man with his dollar. Avarice may be the thorn-root in the poor as in the rich, and it will bring forth as evil a harvest in the one as in the other. Riches promise much of comfort, ease and power; but these do not come without an accompaniment of larger responsibilities and greater dangers, and very frequently the promise is altogether deceptive. How often the appearances deceive one as to the reality! The rich fool in the parable rejoiced in the accumulation of goods for many years, his wealth was the whole of his life, its acquisition and its care absorbed him; but the command of Jehovah, "this night they require of thee thy soul," showed how deceptive his wealth had been. The getting of wealth often becomes a moral disease, corrupting infinitely more valuable things in the life. With all their power to bless, riches are as likely to curse.

"They that are minded to be rich fall into a temptation and a snare and many foolish and hurtful lusts, such as drown men in destruction and perdition." Their minds absorbed in getting money, they lose sight of higher values, and often altogether lose the ability to secure anything but earthly values. Instead of ease and quietness, how often wealth breeds avarice and unholy ambitions working by unholy methods. The excessive haste to be rich leads to methods in business which rapidly destroy permanent moral wealth in order to increase temporary material riches.

Riches are thorns when they rob us of simplicity. Many a man, becoming suddenly rich, has lost his greatest charm of character, and won only the hollow flattery of those who secretly smile at the assumption of the man they pretend to respect. Riches are ever a temptation to prodigality, luxury, and fuller service of mammon. Drawn out of the sight of the woes and needs of others, there is continual danger of a rapid development of gross selfishness, and a loss of sympathy with the poor and the weak. Many have inherited great possessions, only to be cursed with poverty of heart.

Yet no one is more deserving of honor than the rich man who has kept himself unspotted from the stains of undue haste and doubtful methods in acquiring, and from pride and selfishness in possessing. He is worthy of all respect who can receive unharmed the false homage and vile flattery so generally accorded to money. One of the humblest Christians I have ever known was a man accounted rich.

His memory is blessed. Those who knew him best remember and love him for his goodness, not his wealth. The world is full of examples where wealth has proved a blessed minister to the christian life. Thus while riches are often thorns lacerating human hearts, they may be good seed, producing a hundred fold in the heart of him who possesses, and in the lives of those whom he blesses.

But not only are those who become rich in danger of losing their simplicity, but there is even greater danger among those who remain poor. How often the sight of wealth breeds envy, jealousy, and painful discontent. All these are thorns, and of the most dangerous kind. To the rich and to the poor, riches are dangerous chiefly in their deceitfulness, promising so much more than they can give. We give up simplicity because they promise greater comfort in luxury, and greater power in display. And how frequently our hearts are deceived by the promise that as soon as we are rich we will do great good with our money, and thus are tempted to such absorbing haste to be rich that we lose the very capability to fulfill the promise. Generous giving as we are receiving is the only sure way of giving with God's blessing; it may be the only way to avoid dying "wickedly rich."

Riches are thorns when they steal our love from Christ. In days when we had but little, our heart's affections poured in concentrated stream to Christ. For Him we lived. In His presence we thought, and loved, and worked. Riches came and gave us other thoughts and aims. We felt the possession of a new power, and with this increase of influence, our pride grew. We seldom stopped to think how temporary that power was. The love of self began to crowd out the love of Christ. That which lifted us heavenward gave place gradually to that which absorbed us in things that soon must die. Deceived by this new power, we no longer felt the need of divine power. Cheated by the glitter of this new idol, we lost our devotion to God. The sensuous choked out the spiritual, until the heart's fertility was all exhausted to support a growth of weeds that shall at last prevent any of the truth coming to perfection.

Riches are thorns when they lead to pride. Counting our money as part of ourselves, we receive the respect paid to our dollars as if it were reverence paid to our character. A true man will receive respect and honor, whether he be rich or poor. A true man will render respect to nobleness of character wherever he find it, whether amid riches or poverty. It is not wealth that wins for you the companionship and confidence of honest men. The man you may call friend is the one who admires and honors your truthfulness, your uprightness, your christian strength of character. Lose your wealth, and he will still respect and help you, if you still prove yourself a man. Yet how many are proud less of what they are than of what they have.

The eager rush for wealth would lead

one to suppose that it constituted the very highest aim of life. With a vast number everything is sacrificed for money. The best years of life are given to its acquisition. Character is too often put in jeopardy by doubtful ventures. Opportunity of self-culture in what is highest and best is neglected for closer pursuit of riches. By the eagerness of older gold-seekers youth is tempted to turn aside from truth and the slower methods of honest accumulation, to whatever will most quickly fill the coffers. Wealth may be honestly gathered and righteously enjoyed, and the truest Christian may reap largely of this world's harvest, and by every acquisition illustrate pure christian principle; but he must be ever mindful of the command that while he is "diligent in business," he must also be "fervent in spirit," with Godly service.

"*Pleasures of this life.*" Here all are alike, rich and poor, learned and ignorant, for these are the common weeds. They ruin multitudes where riches ruin scores.

Do you remember that young man so active in things good and holy, now so useless to his Master? You know the cause of his failure. He received the word, and it grew rapidly for a time, promising a large harvest. But his Christianity stood in the way of his pleasures, so he crowded out the good seed with a growth of evil weeds. Sinful pleasures kill more souls, and mar the beauty of more christian lives, than all other thorns combined.

Sometimes people are foolish enough to attempt to stifle sorrow by the "pleasures of this life," forgetting that at the same time they may be stifling a nobler life. How much better to purify sorrow with fervent trust in God, making our very affliction "work out for us a far more exceeding and eternal weight of glory."

There is none too much pleasure in this life, but there is a higher use of life than pleasure-seeking, a use that has peace and pleasure in its very nature. Yet how many men and women come gradually to know no higher end of life than "to enjoy themselves," meaning to enjoy everything but themselves. Do they never look up from their self-indulgence with a wish for something richer and nobler? Can they be content to live so valueless a life? All true pleasures have their proper place in the christian life, but out of their own place they are in the way of better things. With the mere pleasure-seeker, inclination controls duty, hence such a man never knows the highest pleasure of christian labor—duty performed for the honor of Christ and the good of other souls.

"LUST OF OTHER THINGS."

Consuming love for any other thing will have the same effect upon the good seed that the "cares of the world" and the "deceitfulness of riches" have. It will not permit the fruit to come to perfection. Such unhallowed love is the root of envy and jealousy. It hears with sorrow of another's prosperity and success, and never wishes good to another without a *proviso*, or a protest of the heart.

Political ambition, as too generally exhibited, has a place under this head. Politics may be, and ought to be, honorable. The politician whose aim is ever to lift his country to its highest possible life, to seek out the needs and possibilities of man's nature and interpret them in laws for his help, deserves high honor. In such labor he is a true minister of God. But when he is a mere seeker of place and individual profit, he is a thorn of the very worst kind. Christianity is a much needed ingredient in our present politics.

The trouble with this third class of hearers is not only in the preparation of the soil, but also in the later cultivation. The weeds not only exhaust the soil of its fertility, but grow up and become a screen between the good seed and the sun. What a false view of the Sun of Righteousness we often get by looking through the shadows of our own weed-grown lives! And sometimes these evil weeds of our hearts grow so thickly and so large that they entirely exclude from our lives the great "light of the world." Their beginnings are almost imperceptible, but their growth is rapid and their fruit deadly. Either we must destroy the weeds, or the weeds will ruin us. In both Peter and Judas there were many thorn-roots; one destroyed them, the other was destroyed by them.

While the good seed is getting a fair start, a wise farmer will go over his field with care to destroy all the weeds and thorns likely to hinder the growth of the good grain. So will a wise hearer of the word watch against the evil weeds and thorns that spring up in our lives so easily and so rapidly.

As we approach from barrenness to the full harvest, we notice that the causes of failure get nearer and nearer to the heart, and are more and more subtle in their character. In the first class, the causes of failure were entirely outward—feet and birds. In the second, both outward and inward—sun and rock. Here the causes are entirely inward—cares, deceitfulness, pleasures.

Outward opposition is overcome, but inward temptation kills them.

The wrong and danger come from allowing these weeds to grow in the heart as if they were of as good quality as the true seed, as if mammon were as good as God. The only proper place for thorns is as a protecting hedge around the field, and the only proper place for cares is on the borders of life as ministers of protection to the more valuable things within.

When you remove a thorn or weed, be sure to sow in its place some good seed. If a large weed in the field is pulled up, it leaves a bare spot, but with loosened soil. If good grain be immediately scattered, a good growth will be produced. If the spot be left to itself, it will either become hard, so that no seed can take root, or evil seeds floating in the air will take possession. Be careful, Christian, how you cultivate your heart's soil and the divine seed which the husbandman has planted there, lest when he gathers the completed harvest of your earthly life, it be for him only a measure of weeds, a crown of thorns.

But who is free from thorns? Emphatically, no one. But the deeper question is, what is your attitude towards them? One of neglect, one of favor, or one of deadly hostility? "Break up your fallow ground, and sow not among thorns."

The fundamental weakness of this class of hearers is that they allow good and evil seeds an equal place in their lives, and thus they are divided against themselves. Their whole life is a conflict. The two crops are struggling for possession of the life, and the end is almost certain to be the death of the good, for the good requires careful cultivation, while the evil grows without any care.

"Keep thy heart with all diligence, for out of it are the issues of life." *Prov.* 4: 23.

> "Create in me a clean heart, O God;
> And renew a right spirit within me."
>
> *Ps.* 51: 10.

"Among the various undertakings of men, can there be mentioned one more important, can there be conceived one more sublime, than an intention to form the mind anew after the Divine Image?"

Coleridge.

FOURTH CLASS OF HEARERS.

" And other fell on good ground, and did yield fruit that sprang up and increased; and brought forth, some thirty, and some sixty, and some an hundred."

Fruitfulness is the mark of difference between this class and all the others. Each of the others bears some resemblance to this class, as error invariably carries a front mask resembling the truth, and it is this surface-appearance of truth that gives to every system of error its time of success.

Like the first class of hearers, this fourth class heard; but unlike them, and like the second class, they received the word. They heeded it, and gladly made it a part of their lives. Yet, unlike the second, and like the third, there was no rock, but abundance of rich soil. Instead of a shallow loosening of the feelings, the whole nature was ploughed, as in the third class. Unlike the third class, however, the old roots were all removed, and dangerous evil seeds floating in the air from neighboring fields of weeds were carefully avoided or destroyed. Continually the heart-field was examined. Evil weeds were pulled up by the roots, and good seed sown in the loosened spots; or, if the evil was not entirely uprooted, the soul stood in an attitude of opposition to every evil thing, while always favoring the good. In every case of failure, the fault lay not with the sower or the seed, not with the sun or the rain, but with the soil. There is an advance throughout the parable, which culminates with this class of fruit-bearers. The members of the first class hear, but do not receive the truth into their lives. Those of the second class hear and gladly cover the new seed with the shallow surface covering of their emotions, but there is no change of character; the heart is only stirred, not changed, hence they quickly die. Those of the third class hear, cover the seed deeply, have no rocks in the way, and really begin a new life, but they allow so many other roots and seeds to grow with the pure seed that they destroy its roots with thirst, and its fruits with thorns and evil shadows. In this fourth class, the word is heard, received into the life's best soil, and bears full fruit. Hard paths are ploughed up, rocks are crushed, and evil seeds and roots of thorns are killed and thrown away. The new life permeates with regenerating power the entire inner nature, while its fruits make beautiful and valuable the whole life of thought and deed. The life of such a hearer is not his old life, but the life of Christ growing in him, and causing him to grow into the likeness of his Lord.

In the wayside hearer there was no life. In the rocky-hearted hearer the seed was only scratched into the surface and had but a temporary life. In the thorny hearer the truth rooted deeply and grew almost to harvest time, but the thorns and weeds prevented the fruit ripening. In this class the seed falls, the roots tap every spring of the heart, its tendrils feel their way through every affection, and its foliage and fruit may be seen in holy thoughts, in words of love, in deeds of righteousness.

Perhaps the most serious difference between the third and fourth classes is that in the fourth the life is united, while in the third the life is trying to serve both God and mammon, trying to raise full crops of both grain and thorns. In the one, all the resources of the life are concentrated to reach one aim. No division is allowed. "But one thing I do, forgetting those things which are behind, and stretching forward (eagerly) to the things which are before, I press on toward the goal unto the prize of the high calling of God in Christ Jesus." In the other class the "house is divided against itself." The good seed springs up and grows rapidly in one set of conditions, while in another the good is hindered, and the evil grows with great rapidity. So a man of the third class may be very religious one day, surrounded by favoring conditions, and very wicked the next day because surrounded by temptations. His life is divided. Climbing to-day and falling to-morrow—making no advance towards "bringing fruit to perfection."

Even in the fourth class the full fruit-bearing is not seen immediately after the reception of the word. The seed must have a sowing, a summer growth, and an autumnal ripeness for gathering.

Let us stand in the Autumn by the reapers as they gather up the harvest.

The hard path is still there. The bare spot and the thorny place are easily found. See the Master look with pity upon the barren, hardened path, and with sorrow upon the dead stalks marking the rocky spot! With what grief of rejected love does He search among the weeds and thorns for any straggling mark of life! Is any gasping, smothered life striving to get the attention of the Lord of the harvest? 'Tis only a leaf, or a shriveled, unripe grain. No fruit brought to perfection. But with what pleasure He looks upon the bowed heads, lowly with their full harvest of perfect grain. Some offer Him a hundred fold, no bare spots, no weeds, no ripened thorns; but a harvest as full and perfect as the life's soil well ploughed and cultivated could produce. Some sixty fold, no weeds or thorns are there; but it may be that before they were rooted out they weakened the soil, and in their place the grain is yet green in harvest time. Some thirty fold, no thorns and a good harvest; but it may be that good seed was not sown while the ground was yet loose after pulling up the weeds and thorns, or the thorns were removed from the life too late for the good seed to grow to a harvest.

"*But that which was sown upon good ground is he that heareth and understandeth.*" "*But that on good ground are they, which in an honest and good heart, having heard the word, keep, and bring forth fruit with patience.*"

It is an honest soil. It is all through to any depth just what it appears to be on the surface, clean and rich. Not only so, but it is a good soil, free from all bad roots and seeds, and perfectly adapted to receive the good seed and produce a harvest. The soil is not good in the sense that the harvest is all ready for the granary. The heart is not good in the sense that it is already righteous, already holy, already perfect and prepared for the heavenly garner. A good heart is one free from all deception. An honest heart is a sincere one. Sincerity, however, is not all that is necessary, Yet how often we hear men say, "It makes little difference what a man believes if he is only sincere." Paul of Tarsus was sincere when he was making havoc of the church; he afterwards proved that his early life was all wrong. The Chinaman worshiping Joss is sincere, yet who is foolish enough to say he is right? The traitor may believe his treason right, yet the government puts him to death notwithstanding his sincerity. A man going southward may sincerely believe that he is on the right road to a city that is really in the north, but will he ever reach his destination unless he forsake his old way, and travel in the opposite direction?

"*An honest and good (noble) heart*" is necessary. Not only a sincere one, but one ready and seeking for the truth. In such a heart the truth finds recognition and a home. The soil is fully ready for it, and the truth is seeking just such a soil. The Master does not say there are no evil roots or thorns growing there. By naming different measures He implies that in part of the soil there was something that reduced the measure from a hundred fold to sixty, and even to thirty. Yet all the soil was honest and good. There may have been thorns in the heart, but there was an honest and sincere effort to eradicate them. Every heart, though capable of producing a hundred fold of the good seed, has in it some roots of evil.

The fertile plain of Babylon, Herodotus tells us, commonly produced two hundred fold. Yet there must have been even in that fertile land some unfruitful spots, and here or there a weed or thorn.

The purest lives are marred by some sins. The most fertile heart has in it some unfruitful spots. Not all the christian graces exhibit a hundred fold increase in any one life. Yet an honest and good heart is ever ready, with eager desire and strong purpose, to receive the seed, and to give it every opportunity to grow. Goodness of heart consists in readiness to receive good seed and refuse evil. An honest and good heart always has a sincere love for the truth, and a fear and hatred of sin.

We are commanded, not to produce a certain measure of fruitfulness, but to bring to perfection the natural harvest of truth. Our work is definite and clear. Not to control the issues of life, but, so far as in us lies, to cleanse and to keep clean the heart-fountain, whence they flow.

It is not in the measure, but only in the kind that we are commanded to bring forth perfection. Three measures of quantity are given in the parable, yet all are called good. The scale of quantity is the capacity of our nature. The standard of quality is similitude with God. The one is as variable as human character. The other as immutable as the Divine Nature. The end is ever the same; progress towards it is in ever varying speed. The kind of the harvest is fixed by the nature of the seed—divine seed must produce divine harvest. And since the quality of the seed and the harvest is fixed by the Divine Husbandman, it is therefore perfect. In quantity, both are dependent upon the heart-soil's capacity to receive and produce. But we have the comfort of the thought that the seed, whose very nature is to live and put forth energy, will surely produce its harvest to the utmost capacity of every life into which it falls. "Keep thy heart with all diligence; for out of it are the issues of life,"—as the grain springs out of a fertile field.

It is possible for a single hearer of the gospel to represent all these four classes in succession, passing from the lowest to the highest in their order. But if he belong to this fourth class, his character will not be a building without plan, a wing added here, a shed there, as the time-need is; but the whole building will be "fitly framed together" and growing toward a perfect plan, the attainment of a God-given ideal. This life and the life of Heaven will not be simply linked together; but both will be built of the same material, woven with the same warp and woof. Both will be the ever-ripening, ever-increasing harvest from the one divine sowing. Death to such a life will be but the throwing down of the scaffold from the completed character-building, the removal of the *débris* for the entrance of the heavenly furniture. It will be but taking the web of life from the loom of earthly struggle, and brushing off the broken threads and mortal dust. It will be but the transplanting of a divine plant, from the exhausted earth-soil, to the broader field of an eternal world. If the two soils have a close resemblance, there will be no shock in the transplanting. But if there be nothing in the earthly soil like the soil of Heaven, how can the life which has grown entirely out of the one get any nourishment from a soil of such opposite character as the other? Heavenly graces grow in earthly soil, but all things earthly die in every attempt to carry them into Heaven.

This character seed produces no selfish harvest. The bloom and the fragrance and the ever-ripening fruit cannot be limited to self. Others will enter within the blessing. "For we are laborers together with God; ye are God's husbandry; God's building." And every laborer with God is moved by the spirit of Him who came "not to be ministered unto, but to minister." Holy is the fragrance of some of these earnest, laborious lives, and many are the golden grains of blessing that fall from them into our weaker and less fruitful hearts. They are "God's building," in whose shade we rest. "God's husbandry," where we gather fruit for refreshment in our weakness and our need. And their number is increasing. The husbandman is ever improving his estate, ploughing up trodden paths, crushing hard rocks, rooting out weeds and thorns, and scattering the perfect seed of His eternal kingdom. Thus that kingdom is ever enlarging. All the causes necessary for its complete establishment and success are at work. The seed is more and more widely sown as the years go by. Richer and more abundant fruits are being produced by the increasing care of heart-culture. Men are gradually perceiving that Christ-likeness is the only true ideal of life, and that grand ideal is more and more prominently coming into contrast with lower aims, and thus dwarfing them still more. The omnipotent and all-wise God is on the throne, and His eternal purpose is to perfect all things in Christ, and through Him to establish the kingdom of heaven as the universal and everlasting kingdom.

The Christian need have no hesitation about scattering the seed, for the word of God has gone forth that it shall not return unto him void. "Sow beside all waters," is the urgent command of the Lord of the harvest, and implicit obedience is only faithfulness to duty. Christian, your own life depends, in a very large degree, upon your faithfulness in sowing seed for growth in other lives. And yet while you sow, remember the influence of your own life in winning for the seed a good reception. Sow as the Master sowed, with longing love and ceaseless prayer.

Remember that your life is more the exposition of your heart than of your head. You may think the right and live the wrong. You may think the truth, and understand its deepest statements, and yet live in profoundest error and evil. But what your heart loves profoundly, supremely, will, sooner or later, be expressed in your life, and the world believes when the life speaks. Conversion is not change of habit, but change of the very principle of life. And change of principle is not change of opinion, but of loves and motives that come from the heart, not the head.

And as ye go forth to sow, remember the words of the Master, "Lo, I am with you alway, even to the end of the world." Be not disheartened with the failures in the three classes, for here and there a good and honest heart will receive the word and multiply your sowing sixty or a hundred fold.

"Keep thy heart with all diligence, for out of it are the issues of life." *Prov.* 4: 23.

"In order to learn, we must attend; in order to profit by what we have learnt, we must think—that is, reflect. He only thinks who reflects." "It is worthy of special observation, that the Scriptures are distinguished from all other writings pretending to inspiration, by the strong and frequent recommendations to knowledge, and a spirit of inquiry. Without reflection, it is evident that neither the one can be acquired nor the other exercised."

Coleridge.

"*Take heed what ye hear.*" (Mark 4: 24.) "*Take heed how ye hear.*" (Luke 8: 18.)

This is a very important admonition, yet we pay very little attention to it. How many of us are watchful to hear only that which will help us to a nobler life? "*What ye hear.*" Words of wisdom and words of sinful folly are ever competing for our attention, trying to reach the mind, not only through the ear, but through the eye from printed page and picture. In a thousand forms of appeal trying to get our attention, and influence our life.

What a motley group of petitioners they are that plead for a hearing! Some coming laden with gold and all manner of wholesome spices, royal gifts to enrich us with things that are good and pure; others bringing deadly poisons with which to steal away our senses while they rob us of the true wealth and beauty of our lives. Some come to teach us a higher harmony of life, to attune us to full accord with God's most holy will; others would woo us to sin by strains that can at last leave us only with discordant sorrow and remorse.

Many a soul has received its first stain in some heedless hearing, when every door of approach to the mind should have been carefully guarded, and every word that approached the ear, and every page that came before the eye, compelled to pass a challenging scrutiny as to their value and their purpose. Many a child is stained and weakened for life by the careless permission of parents and teachers. They do not wish it, but they do not guard against it.

Heedlessness as to what we hear is our first danger, but the admonition concerning it is not more important than the second, "Take heed *how* ye hear." We are not only heedless as to what we hear, but we are careless how we hear what is good. Many a follower of Christ, who is weak to-day, might soon grow strong by careful attention to this command, and all of us would find it wholesome food for faith and peace.

The parable indicates at least three conditions of profitable hearing of the word of the kingdom.

First,—*Attention.*

The reason why the wayside hearer received no benefit from the truth was because he did not understand it. And he did not understand it because, when he heard the word, he did not attend to it, did not study it, did not concentrate the powers of his mind upon it to know its full meaning. Inattention was the cause of death to all the truth that had fallen upon his heart. "*Take heed how ye hear,*" is an all-important injunction, for careless hearing, cynical hearing, attention to the form instead of the truth, receiving the husk instead of the seed, is the secret of a vast deal of the church's weakness. Attention is more than a mere hearing of words; it is attending to them in order to know their full meaning, their purpose in relation to self, and their fullest value to the life.

"*Having heard, keep, and bring forth fruit with patience.*" "*Keep!*" A student hearing a valuable truth says, "I must *keep* that." How does he do it? By concentrating his attention upon it until it becomes a part of himself. He looks at it on every side to see all its phases. He does not simply think how valuable or how beautiful it is, but absorbs it into his very life.

But more than attention is necessary to profitable hearing. The second class of hearers gave full attention to the "word," and received it into willing hearts; but it brought forth no fruit in the harvest because there was no true preparation of the heart for hearing the gospel; it was a mere surface reception.

Therefore, second, *preparation* is necessary.

The second class died because the preparation was not thorough. A hearer may pay close attention to the truth, fully assenting to it in his mind, and gladly receiving it in his heart; but if there is not a complete breaking up of the old rock of sin, the new life—which requires for its full growth all of a man's nature—will die before the summer of his life is over. Not only must the ploughing be deep and thorough, but the old roots of sin must be pulled up and thrown away from the life. Sorrow for sin must grow into a hatred of sin and a righteous fear of it. The true loves of the heart must be purified and strengthened by companionship with divine love, while unholy affections must be cut off from all congenial companionship, and fought against until dead or completely in subjection to a will that is allied only with pure affections.

But something more is necessary than attention and preparation. The third class of hearers both gave attention and received the word into soil prepared for its growth, but there was no fruit brought to perfection.

Third,—*Cultivation* is necessary.

An honest and good hearer of the word is in earnest. With him, hearing is an important matter. Not to beguile an hour, or fulfill a duty, but to enlarge and enrich his life. It is a part of life's supremest question, out-ranking in importance every other interest, whether of business, of family, or of reputation. To him, everything else is secondary to his permanent, eternal life. Hence he not only listens earnestly, honestly and patiently; but is a "sincere doer of the word." To him, religion is not merely opinion, or theory, or knowledge; it is life eternal, and therefore he cannot rest content with merely ploughing and sowing, but must cultivate with all skill and care that the harvest may be abundant and of the very best quality.

Whatever care may be taken in the preparation of the soil and in the sowing, all the weeds and thorn-roots cannot be entirely removed before the seed begins to grow, and with the good growth the evil that is left in the soil will surely spring up. If the husbandman is watchful and industrious, these evil roots may be removed before doing much harm; but while life lasts there is danger. Old sins which you thought were entirely eradicated long ago, may spring up again to choke your better life. Therefore the Master bids all to "watch and pray" against every evil thing. There is especial value in this third injunction, for whatever we love becomes a theme of our thoughts, enters into the formation of our ideal of life, and modifies all our plans. Every object of our love draws us towards its own likeness in proportion to the strength of the affection. The only way to avoid becoming like what we love is to sacrifice the affection. Christ is Jehovah's ideal for all our race. We reach the highest possible attainment in life when we arrive at the full stature of Christ. If we love Him supremely, love Him for His purity, His divine greatness of character, love Him as the ideal for our own life, we shall grow like Him. Our present life is the soil. "The word of the kingdom" is the seed. Eternal perfection, likeness to Christ, is the ripened harvest of our life. It is worth all it costs to prepare the soil thoroughly, and cultivate it with watchful industry, in order that so divine a seed may produce a full harvest.

Take four boys sitting together at school and watch their careers. One is stupid; he hears with indifference. Truth makes no impression on him. He is a mere wayside hearer.

The second boy is bright, quick, probably the smart boy of the school and the pride of his home. He hears and instantly lays hold of the truth taught,—his whole countenance tells that he has caught the meaning. His recitation is brilliant, but it is seed very near the surface, no depth. Anyone who will tickle the surface will get a quick, bright response; but such a boy never gets beyond the reputation or the ability of his school days. A few years out of school, and he becomes commonplace, disappointing many great expectations.

The third boy hears, studies the matter in all its bearings, lays strong hold of it, understands it, and absorbs it into his life. He can never forget it. It is become a part of him. But he absorbs all other instruction just as thoroughly. That things are contradictory makes little difference as to the place he gives them in his life. He may become an encyclopædia of information, but it always remains information, never becomes life. He stands in the same attitude towards one kind of knowledge as towards another. His distinctions are not clearly drawn. He is full of all manner of goods, a "curiosity shop" of ideas and beliefs, but there is a great scarcity of convictions. Erasmus was a very able scholar, but there were too many weeds in his heart, and the driving Reformation tide pushed him aside and left him stranded alone. Luther with less knowledge, but with mighty convictions, moved all Europe, and kept his place at the very front of the Reformation till the end of his life.

Our fourth boy will hear as the third, and with no more thorough knowledge, but while he masters fundamental truths, he also cultivates his susceptibility to every impression of like truth. He learns to recognize the lineaments of truth, and accepts only that information which can stand harmonious adjustment with what he already knows to be true. His knowledge may be as vast and varied as his friend's, but he stands in an altogether different relation to it. He cultivates a love for all that is true, and as carefully cultivates a hatred for whatever is false. His convictions grow with his knowledge, and his attitude is conscientiously uncompromising. It is not enough that we hear the truth and "keep it," but we must keep it clean from all association with evil.

The whole duty of hearing may be summed up in these two commands, "Take heed *what* ye hear," and, "Take heed *how* ye hear." Hear the truth, and take heed how ye hear it. Avoid all else than truth. Hear not falsehood, hear not folly, hear not evil. Hear the truth, "the word of the kingdom," at all hazard, but take heed how ye hear even the truth. Hear it with attention, with due preparation of heart, and with continued cultivation, for this is the hearing by which faith comes, "and by grace are ye saved through faith."

"And that which thou sowest, thou sowest not to that body that shall be, but bare grain it may chance of wheat, or of some other grain:

But God giveth it a body as it hath pleased Him, and to every seed His own body."—*I Cor.* 15: 37, 38.

>   Ah! when shall all men's good
> Be each man's rule, and universal peace
> Lie like a shaft of light across the land,
> And like a lane of beams athwart the sea,
> Through all the circle of the golden year?
> *   *   *   *   *   *
> "As if the seedsman, rapt
> Upon the teeming harvest, should not dip
> His hand into the bag: but well I know
> That unto him who works, and feels he works,
> This same grand year is ever at the doors"
> —*Tennyson.*

"We have attempted to produce facts and evidence which should make it probable, that by far the greatest factor in the moral and humane progress of mankind, is the influence of the person and teachings of Jesus Christ. The argument is logical; and whoever overthrows it, cannot do so by vague declamation, but only by presenting a sufficient cause, other than Christianity, which shall account for these facts and changes."—"*Gesta Christi.*"

PARABLE OF GROWTH.

"And He said, So is the kingdom of God, as if a man should cast seed into the ground;

And should sleep, and rise night and day, and the seed should spring and grow up, he knoweth not how.

For the earth bringeth forth fruit of herself; first the blade, then the ear; after that, the full corn in the ear.

But when the fruit is brought forth, immediately He putteth in the sickle, because the harvest is come."—(Mark 4: 26-29.)

This parable, so full of seed for the Christian life, so rich in its hints of the nature of spiritual growth, and so helpful in its prophecy of the final harvest, is an appropriate theme for a Spring-time study.

The Parable of the Sower taught us how the good seed was scattered by the

Sower, and how it was received by human hearts. This parable teaches the nature of the seed, the character of its growth, and the certainty of the harvest. In both parables, the "field is the world," and the seed is "the word of the kingdom." In the former, the "harvest is the end of the world;" in the latter, the harvest is when "the fruit is brought forth (or offers itself)."

The parable of sowing taught us that while the good seed was to be scattered freely everywhere, whatever the quality of the soil, in many lives it would bring forth no ripened harvest. In this parable it is assumed that good seed cast into good ground will grow to its proper harvest, while the main purpose of the parable is to illustrate the inherent vitality and productiveness of the seed, and the progressive character of its growth to perfection.

For our analysis we cannot do better than to follow the order of thought given in the parable.

"*As if a man should cast seed into the ground.*"

There is a suggestion here worth careful attention, but as it is not necessary to an exposition of the parable, and to avoid repetition, it will be considered in our study of the law of sowing and reaping.

"*And should sleep and rise night and day.*"

Seed-time and harvest are the two prominent seasons in a farmer's life. All things else in his work are secondary to the sowing and the reaping, hence in the Master's parable they are left in the background. The soil is to be carefully prepared, the evil weeds thrown out, the poisonous roots destroyed, and good seed cast into the ground. The less important things are necessary, and therefore the sower does not sit down in idleness after the sowing, but does whatever is necessary to prepare for the coming harvest. So far as the growth of the seed is concerned, he can do nothing but wait. He knows "not how" it grows, but rests in the certainty that by a natural law, not under his control, the seed will grow to the harvest.

This is not a doctrine that permits indolence, but a lesson of patience and hope. When a man has done his wisest work with all thoroughness and skill, he has dealt only with the *conditions* of growth. He cannot give to the seed any additional power to "spring up and grow." His work is altogether with the outward conditions, not at all with the inward life. All he can do is to take the seed which has life in itself, and put it in the ground which has the fertility to support that life in its growth, then patiently and hopefully to wait for the harvest. He may know very little of the laws of growth, but he is very sure of the fact of growth; and hence his patience comes not from ignorance of the manner, but from assurance of the fact.

How slow we are to learn this lesson of patience that is taught with so great sublimity in every work of God, and with so great emphasis in all His word. No one can read the story of that long period when Jehovah was drawing the present sublime harmony of the universe out of its early confusion and darkness, without wondering at the infinite patience of the Creator. He planted the seeds of the future harvest of beauty and order, and then let them grow according to the principle of life which He had put within them. The growth of continents, of trees, and of animal life, and the slow development of human history, tell the same story of the patience of our God.

The Bible teaches even more plainly the unhasting patience of Jehovah in working out his mighty designs. The lives of His ancient prophets, Enoch, Noah, Abraham, Moses, were all illustrations of His patient sowing and waiting for a harvest. The whole course of human history is an illustration of Jehovah's patience with a sinful, rebellious people, yet He never falters in His efforts to bring them up to the height of His eternal purpose for their redemption. How patiently the

Saviour laid the deep, enduring foundations of His kingdom! He knew truth's power of growth, and, therefore, without fear or doubt, waited for the harvest. What patience to go quietly on through shame to death without once trying to hasten the end, or resist the cruelty!

The Christian's view of time and life should come from his Lord, who counted the earthly life of worth mainly as a Springtime for the sowing of "the word of the kingdom," with all eternity for the growth. We think of time in periods, as its beats its changes into our lives, but there are no such divisions of time with God. He who was before time began, and still will be when time is ended, has no need to count its years or note its changing history. The end, the beginning, and all the history are present to His consciousness; hence He never unwisely hurries, or indolently lags; but always moves in patience from the first cause in Himself through all the infinite variety of growth and wide-branching effects to His own final purpose.

Definitely, certainly, persistently, by the principle of growth which He has put within all life, and the command He lays upon it, Jehovah is guiding our whole race to the final harvest. Yet how often He might say to us as he said to Ephraim of old, "I took them on My arms; but they knew not that I healed them."

In our impatience to see the end of wickedness, we sometimes forget that the "times and seasons" are in God's hand, and are tempted even to lose our faith in His supreme control of all the issues of life. We cry out, less in prayer than in unbelief, "How long, O Lord, how long!" And sometimes we even try to gather the harvest before it is ripe, and thus in our "zeal without knowledge" ruin all.

A few years before the civil war, Fred. Douglass was addressing a crowded audience. He depicted the fearful condition of his race, the degradation and horrors of slavery, the indifference of one great political party, and the determined opposition of the other. The Supreme Court had just decided against the black man, and all the indications seemed to point to a heavier curse than ever about to fall upon his doomed race. The picture was a fearful one, and it oppressed the audience with the speaker's own feelings of despair, and they were ready with him to cry out for vengeance. In a moment of profound silence, that strange old woman, Sojourner Truth, rose from her seat, and pointing her bony finger at the speaker, asked, "Frederick, is God dead?" It was like a flash of light in midnight gloom. In his own way and time, Jehovah made His purpose plain.

The best we can do is to do our best, and then to "hope and quietly wait," leaving the harvest all to God. Our discouragement grows out of lack of faith, just as hopelessness always follows the death of faith. We may look over the world and see only the very apparent fruits of sin in the church, and see only its parsimony and lack of fidelity to the great trust for which it exists; but such a view is thoroughly deceptive. Like the cynic's view of a sincere and earnest life, we carry to a great problem a little mind, and hastily condemn as not existing a power of life too rich and deep for our narrow souls to measure. Like the leaven in the meal, like the seed beneath the soil, secretly and certainly, the "mind that was in Christ" is taking possession of the intellectual and spiritual life of our world.

This influence is creeping into the world's legislation, into social customs, into war and commerce, into heathen lands and heathen hearts, and everywhere it is growing towards the full possession of the world for Christ. It is the quiet whisper of God to all our race, saying, "This is the way, walk ye in it, when ye turn to the right hand and when ye turn to the left." This ought to put to death all thought of our own importance, and make us feel a deep humility in the presence of truth with its endless life and mighty work. Christ sowed and Christ shall reap. For there are two great seasons in the life of His kingdom, when He was here to sow and when He comes again to reap. Between these times is the silent, secret growth of the kingdom under the guidance of the Spirit. Our work is to scatter the seed, and wait for the harvest.

"And the seed shall spring up and grow, he knoweth not how."

Christ evidently expected His kingdom to have a perfectly natural growth; rapid and wonderful, but strictly according to the law of growth; and any careful study of this parable will disclose a very close analogy between growth in nature and growth in the spiritual kingdom.

All the phenomena of growth are indications of a profound mystery. Every farmer is sure that his seed is growing; he can point out all the marks of growth; but "he knoweth not how" it grows. Not only is it out of our power to make the seed grow, but it is out of our knowledge how it grows.

From seed through the tender "blade, then the ear, then the full corn in the ear," to the harvest. The outer forms of growth are plain enough, but the inner spirit of life is a profound mystery. And you cannot get away from the mystery; it is everywhere. What is the difference between living tissue and dead? One is a marvellous combination of strength and beauty, perfectly fulfilling its purpose; the other is worthless, except as a study. Man recognizes the fact of difference, but "knoweth not how" this difference is created. As in material growth, so in spiritual, the cause and much of the process are mysterious. The kingdom of spiritual life, like the kingdom of physical life, cometh not with observation, but groweth in secret. "The wind bloweth where it listeth; thou hearest the voice thereof, but knowest not whence it cometh, and whither it goeth: so is everyone that is born of the Spirit."

The spiritual forces at work in the world do not challenge attention by noise or display, yet they are growing into every nook and corner of human life. They may not always completely change a man's heart and mind, but where in all the world is there a spot not already modified by the spiritual forces started by Christ? The Master himself gives us a perfect illustration of this secret and gradual changing of the whole world which He is working by His spirit. He said, "The kingdom of heaven is like unto leaven, which a woman took and hid in three measures of meal, till it was all leavened." Leaven, yeast, is essentially different from the meal into which it is put. So is the kingdom of heaven, the Christ-given life, is a life essentially different from the life of the world, which has no more power to change itself than the meal has to rise without the leaven. It is the principle of new life in Christ that raises the world, completely renewing it, as it is the principle of new life in the leaven that transforms the meal. In both cases it is the life that is introduced, and life that propagates itself secretly and gradually until the "whole lump" is changed.

Science has taught us that the yeast we use is a mass of living cells so minute that "a cubic inch of yeast in the heat of fermentation contains upwards of eleven hundred millions of them." These minute cells, when they grow to full size, give off little buds. These buds in their turn grow and produce other buds. Thus, by a very rapid process of multiplication, this life, which has been put into the heart of the dough, works its way in a few hours to every particle of the whole lump.

"So is the kingdom of heaven." Its seed of life by a gradual, and in a large measure secret, growth, multiplies and spreads until it permeates the whole intellectual and moral life of our race. "The truth" takes men as they are and lifts them to a sanctified life by its own power of growth. Men are not transformed in order to receive the truth, but they receive it in order to be transformed. They cannot transform themselves without the seed of truth any more than the meal can without the leaven.

Thus the task set before the disciples was to sow the seed of truth. They had no power to control its growth, but they had the promise which God has written so often in His book and so plainly in the seed's own life, "It shall not return unto me void; but it shall accomplish that which I please, and it shall prosper in that for which I sent it."

When we contrast the weakness of the men chosen for the work and the enormous difficulties to be overcome, with the rapid spread of the gospel and the wonderful growth of the church, we have a sublime illustration of this parable of the Master.

Secrecy and spontaneity (automate) are attributes of all true growth, whether in the physical world or the spiritual. Not all the marks of growth are on the surface of the field of grain, and we are in serious error if we think that there are no marks of spiritual growth but such as are plain to our eyes. Indeed, it is very doubtful whether the truest spiritual life is ever the most apparent. Many that seem to us to be first, may be last in the Master's judgment. "The word of the kingdom" is not something that is cast away from God, with a life dependent upon the care of men. It is a living spiritual power in which God works to save the immortal souls of beings created in His image. His spirit is the life within the seed of truth, and, therefore, it has an inherent life that compels growth wherever the seed falls into soil capable of supporting life. The seed is not the life, but the means by which the life grows to its own harvest. The life bursts from the seed, leaving it to die, and grows out of the form of one seed through the stalk into a larger and more abundant life in many seeds. The harvest is easily identified with the seed sown, but the life of the little grain has built for itself a larger and more valuable place for itself and its work. Both seed and harvest are reservoirs of the life that has grown from the smaller into the larger. A chemist can make a grain of wheat corresponding exactly in all its parts to the living grain, but the manufactured grain will neither rise with the yeast nor grow in the earth. Man may make the reservoir, but God only can give life. Yet the life is what gives the seed its whole value. So it is with the "word of the kingdom," in external form it may bear the closest resemblance to any word of man; but its inherent life makes it an altogether different seed in both kind and power. Even of the word of God it is said, "The letter (the mere form) killeth"—leads only to death—but the inherent spirit is life. As in the Old Testament the spirit of life grew by means of an elaborate ritual and the words of inspired prophets, so in the New Testament the "word of the kingdom" is the means by which the same spirit is spreading a divine life throughout the world. "The word of God is living, and puts forth energy (growth)."

The power of Judaism over the thoughts

and feelings of the first Christians, the gigantic power in Roman heathenism, the deadly hatred of a world-wide paganism, the subtle opposition of all forms of philosophy, the corrupt ideas almost universally associated with religious worship, the actual denial of the immortality of the soul by the head of the church in ancient Rome a few years before the birth of Christ, the weakness and obscurity of the early Christians, everything seemed to make it impossible for the "kingdom of heaven" to take possession of the world, or even to find a quiet spot in which to keep alive the Christ-taught faith. But in spite of opposition without and ignorance and sin within, the Master's kingdom has gone from victory to victory, persistently growing into possession of the life of the world. We know not how, for we cannot trace it except in the indications that are upon the surface, "the blade, the ear, and the full corn in the ear." We know that the Son of Man scattered the seed, and we saw the tender blade break through the ground only to meet the storms that beat upon it with such relentless fury. Again and again we watched to see it die under the overwhelming opposition of its enemies, and the selfishness and treachery of its friends; but still it grew by its own inherent life, from the tender blade to the ear, and now the full corn in the ear is proving its ability to fulfill the mission inherent in its life, to fill the whole earth with the knowledge of the glory of God.

"*First the blade, then the ear, then the full corn in the ear.*"

These words teach the most important lesson of the parable. "Heaven is not reached by a single bound," any more than a harvest is ready as soon as the sowing is accomplished. Growth there must be from seed to ripened fruit. So with the kingdom of Christ, whether in the world at large, or in the individual life, it must grow, and its usual growth is not fitful, but steadily progressive. Yet from the beginning, when the disciples asked, " wilt Thou at this time restore the kingdom?" even until now, men have ever been looking for "signs and wonders" in spiritual growth.

Yet the Master teaches the law of gradual progress as the law of His kingdom's growth, and every christian student of human history is impressed with the power of this persistent and gradual growth of Christ's influence. A few men of no influence, and not remarkable for either intellectual or spiritual power, are commissioned to sow the seed of a spiritual kingdom. They only half understand their mission, yet are forced from one stage of growth to another, until the ignorant fishermen of Galilee are become the saints of Christendom. So with the seed they scattered; it has grown into possession of the world's best soil, and still is growing with ever increasing vigor.

Like the leaven and the seed, this kingdom of divine life is growing quietly with a sure and gradual growth through the "whole lump" of human life. Trace any of the noblest thoughts and works of to-day to their origin, and you will find that the spirit of Christ has been with them from their birth, giving them their life, and controlling them in their growth.

Take out of our civilization all that has grown directly from Christ's life and teachings, and you would rob the world of its noblest life and greatest beauty. All the inspiring hopes and satisfying faiths born of the Spirit, all the peace of Christ which has quieted so many troubled souls, all that deliverance from the thraldom of creatures to the freedom of children given us by the gospel of redemption, all would be swept away before the storms of passion, and the slavery of sin.

Because we do not see the power of Christ break forth like a human power, but only know it as growing secretly and gradually, is no reason for discouragement. The silent force of gravity is mightier far than the loudest tempest; and the persistent life that to-day is silently urging its way to the harvest in every field, has proven itself stronger than all the storms and bitter cold of winter.

Not "with observation," but in silent, endless growth. Not challenging attention by a storm or flood, but in silent growth within the heart, a well of living water flowing on forever with spiritual life and health in every drop. As in the world at large, so in the individual soul, the kingdom of heaven is like a seed springing into life secretly, and gradually growing to the full harvest Not many of us know how or when the first seed fell into our life, or when the first blade appeared. Just as all the richest things in life "come to us," we know not how or why, so this new life often comes. A blessed gift of God, but why to us, and how did it find a place to grow? Like the love of God which passeth knowledge, we know the gift is ours to use and to enjoy; why it came and how, we leave to God.

The growth of the "kingdom of heaven" in any one human life is as mysterious, secret and progressive, as in a world. We can measure the growth of the kingdom in the world by long periods, but in the individual we have only a few years. In the one the very greatness of the phenomena challenges our attention and helps our understanding of them; but in an individual life we need to look with closer scrutiny, for the time is short and the field is small.

In any study of human progress, one very important thing is to be kept in mind,—the highest powers are of slowest growth. There are so few possible exceptions to this rule that it is doubtful whether it is ever violated. The lowest forms of life grow quickly to their end, and development becomes slower as you rise in the scale of being. In man's own life the physical body reaches its full size and ability in a very few years; the mind requires a longer period for its highest development, while the spiritual growth requires more than all of this life, and we know not yet its range of growth in the world to come. This may be because the physical life is temporary and the spiritual life everlasting, while the intellectual life, partaking of the natures of both physical and spiritual life, is above the one and below the other. Or it may be that the longer time is needed for the higher quality and value of the life lived and the work performed. It takes but a moment to prepare a pane of common window-glass, but months to complete a lense for the telescope. It needs but a little time to train the ear to the simpler musical sounds, but years of careful attention to enjoy the deeper and richer harmonies. It is easy work to gather a great array of facts, but a greater thing and much more difficult to go down into the depths of their meanings, and find their deepest principles. It is a comparatively easy thing to make an open confession of faith in Christ; but it requires years of spiritual growth to be able to find the deep, unchanging principle of the Christ's life and make it the controlling power in one's own life. It is so much easier to follow the Master in outward act than in inward motive. And this is but saying that it is so much easier to do than to be, and the command is not do perfectly, but "*be* ye perfect."

In the individual life we know not how or when the seed first fell and began its growth. We may be able to tell when we first noticed it growing and felt it to be our own new life, but even this is not possible to us all, so gradual has been the growth. The secrecy of the germination and first growth is as marked in a single life as in the larger field of the world, because it is an essential law of growth to spring up secretly, and press noiselessly "towards the mark for the prize" of its high calling, the full and ripened harvest. The world instinctively doubts a loud profession of faith or the appearance of too rapid growth, and half expects it to be blasted by some untimely frost, or early tempest.

Every true spiritual seed must bring forth fruit of itself; we cannot put the fruits upon it, and every act of forcing is apt to be an interference with a higher power at work, and therefore apt to hinder the growth and delay the harvest. It is but childish continually to disturb the seed to see whether it is growing. The lesson we need to learn is taught us in the Master's work with His first disciple. What patience and hopefulness! How slow of growth they were, and yet He was ever prophesying a great harvest from their sowing. Ah, but He saw the future, and knew how successful their work would be! Did He not also foresee the sure growth and abundant fruitfulness of the truth, and has he not taught us over and over again that the seed of truth, "the word of the kingdom," once growing in the "good and honest" heart, cannot die, but must bring forth a harvest "after its kind?" "Be ye patient, therefore, until the coming of the Lord. Behold the husbandman waiteth for the precious fruit of the earth, being patient over it, until it receive the early and latter rain. Be ye also patient; establish your heart; for the presence of the Lord is at hand."

The seed must spring up and grow of itself through the clods and stones of our rough natures, with no more attention from us than is consistent with the perfect freedom of the spiritual life growing silently within us. It is ours to remove the weeds, guard against all enemies, keep our nights cloudless that the dew may fall, and our days uncovered to the full shining of the Sun of Righteousness, and then to put our trust in the new-born endless life within, begotten of Him who "will perfect it until the day of Jesus Christ."

What a light of hope and faith to shine in upon all our anxious fears and doubts! We long and pray and work, and yet feel hopeless. Have we not forgotten the growing power of the truth? Judging by the external appearances, we sometimes forget that the "inner man" may be growing with a power and beauty that only occasionally appear in the outer life.

Conversion, as much as regeneration,

must be a fact in every christian life, but it is not always traceable. Many of us cannot tell the time of our conversion, and many more are in danger of a serious mistake when they count some particular stirring of their emotions as the time, and fact, of their conversion. Most of us can tell when we realized the fact, but even this sometimes comes so gradually as to make it impossible to fix upon any particular hour as the time when we were turned completely round toward God. Yet whether dates and occasions can be traced with certainty or not, if the truth has germinated and put forth its own growth, a real change has begun in the life. And it is not merely a change of thought, or of purpose, but a real change of character. It is a new life, whose legitimate harvest is a perfected character. It is not that completed harvest of life, but it is the springing up of the blade; the ear will follow, and the full harvest shall come according to God's law of spiritual growth.

The feeble blade, tested as it grows, becomes in due time the strong and fruitful harvest; but the new-born life is just as true a life as it ever can be. The first faint love growing through patient service, the ardent enthusiasm becoming hopeful endurance, the early gladness deepening to abiding joy, the buoyancy living on into quietness and peace—this is not change, but development. It is the true and natural growth of the soul. The inner principle is not weaker, nor the outer beauty less, but both are grown into truer harmony and higher fruitfulness. And this last it is that indicates the approach of harvest, and proves the nature of the growth, "By their fruits ye shall know them." The blade and the ear are as truly alive as the ripened grain, but are not yet able to give life in reproduction. They receive, absorb, in order to ripen and reproduce their fruits, and their life is the same as when at last, more fully grown, they give forth their fruits to the husbandman.

We must not expect fruit immediately from the sowing, for we need to remember that in the spiritual kingdom, as in the natural, we have all the phenomena of growth. Sometimes, instead of a long period of gradual growth, there is a very rapid development, as if the forces of life were under some unusual pressure. The manifestations of life are not alike in all who truly live, although the laws of life remain the same. Some, as the tender blade of grass or grain, may not realize the rich store of life within them until the grain is almost ready for the harvest. Others, as the fruit-tree blossoming, immediately challenge attention to the vigor and beauty of their new life. The one reaching its highest beauty and value together in an abundant harvest, the other passing through beauty to the more valuable reproductive fruitfulness.

"*The ear*," between the blade and the harvest, between the blossom and the ripe fruit. This is a dangerous time to many a true christian soul. He has lost the vividness of his first spiritual experiences, and begins to doubt the fact of his conversion, and often mourns the decadence of his spiritual life. There may be good reason for his anxiety, but we must not forget that a natural growth leads through a period of green fruit of bitter taste, when there is neither beauty of blossom nor ripeness of fruit. The green grain may not be as beautiful as the blossom, but it is of greater value because nearer the harvest. To pass out of a first stage of vivid experiences to a time of dullness, and even of questioning; from the early joy to the quiet, perhaps stubborn, endurance of storms and resistance of enemies; may be only a hiding within the sheltering husk for a surer growth. The blade must grow through the green ear to the full harvest, and yet we sometimes distress our souls with a charge of decline when we are really in higher stage of growth.

But we must not hide from ourselves the special dangers of this stage of christian life. For as the grain, when green in the ear, is in danger from unfavorable condition of weather, and from all manner of insects that would feed upon and kill it, so in the spiritual growth this is a time of especial danger from doubt and fear. But we must not think there is no fruit of the Spirit in us because we do not find any of it fully ripe. This is the time when the Husbandman is most patient with us, expecting of us only a careful guarding of the life He has given us, while it grows to the harvest.

It may not be amiss to notice some of these conditions which are within our control. The seed is planted, and has life within itself. The soil "spontaneously bringeth forth fruit;" its powers of sustaining the seed are in its original endowment. The rain and the atmosphere, the sunshine and the night, of this earthly life, will all attend the growing spirit with their various ministry. Our work is not with their production, but with our reception of them, our attitude towards them. We are to make all things without us minister to the new life within us, thus transforming the temporary into sustenance for the eternal. This cannot be done by giving all our attention to these external conditions, nor by looking only at our hearts to watch the growth, but far more by "looking unto Him who is the author and finisher of our faith." For a man does not grow God-like by studying only, or even largely, what he is in himself,—this is to mould his ideal and receive his impulse from himself; but by much patient thought of God and God's ideal for man, does he grow.

Richard Baxter, in his autobiography, expressed this thought perfectly when he said: "I was once wont to meditate most on my own heart, and to dwell all at home and look little higher. I was still poring either on my sins or my wants, or examining my sincerity; but now, though I am greatly convinced of the need of heart acquaintance, yet I see more of a higher work; that I should look oftener upon Christ, and God, and heaven, than upon my own heart I would have one thought at home upon myself and sins, and many thoughts above upon the high, and amiable, and beautifying objects..... I am more solicitous about my duty to God, and less solicitous about His dealings with me."

"But when the fruit is ripe, straightway he putteth forth the sickle, because the harvest is come."

This is the last touch of the parable, and it is full of power and beauty. "Is ripe," literally, offers itself, delivers itself up to the husbandman, as if pressing forward to the next stage of its development. The grain is not merely an article of food to nourish life, but also a seed to reproduce its own life in larger measure. How natural that it should be eager to go forward on its mission. It has passed through all the stages of growth in obedience to the decree written within its own nature, and now returns its fruits to the husbandman for whatever use he may have for them.

It is not more natural for a head of wheat fully ripe to drop its grains into the soil about the stalk, than it is for a ripe christian spirit to drop the seeds of life into neighboring minds and hearts. The harvest is come whenever the grain is ripe. So it is in the kingdom of Christ, not waiting for the end of the world, but giving forth seed as fast as it is ripe, until at length the whole character, fully ready, is gathered into the heavenly garner.

In thinking of the harvest referred to in the Parable of the Sower, the fearful imagery of the fourteenth chapter of Revelation is forced upon the mind; but in this parable, the continual ripening and ever-increasing abundance of the harvest recall the prophecy of Amos, "Behold the days are coming, saith the Lord, that the ploughman shall overtake the reaper, and the treader of grapes him that soweth seed." So vast will be the field to be cultivated, so rapid the growth and so abundant the harvest, that seed-time and harvest will be as one. How true this is of the Master's kingdom! In every field, sowing and reaping go side by side. Indeed, in every life this is true; for what Christian, who really lives, fails to sow even while he is reaping? Of all the grains that fall into his life, none nourish him more than those he scatters abroad to bless other lives.

Every true harvest delivers itself willingly to the husbandman, needing no forcing; but the unripe grain cannot be beaten from its husk, selfishly refusing to give itself forth for another harvest. Lives that are not ripe enough to deliver their spiritual fruits spontaneously, may need cultivation, perhaps a little urging, in order to aid their growth; but forcing is always dangerous. Yet in our impatience to enlarge the harvest, we are tempted to force unripe grain into the sowing, while the life is yet "in the ear," needing all its powers for receiving strength to grow—unnaturally compelling it to reproduce. A forced plant is very apt to be a frail one. Nor must we think that the full harvest can be gathered in this life. The life for which we have sown is endless, and the fruits are too rich and abundant to be all gathered on earth. Immortal life is too vast to give forth in this temporary world anything more than a few indications of its nobility and wealth. Heaven is heaven to us because of what we are becoming, not simply a beautiful home for what we are in this life. Having the power of immortal life within our souls, we look for nothing less than endless growth. Having the image of God born again within our spirits, we will not lower our ideal to anything less than perfection in His likeness,—perfect as God in kind of life, and in degree of likeness ever growing.

How can we become discouraged, with this word of the Master in our minds!

Souls endowed with endless life, heaven and likeness to God as the goal to be reached, and truth with inherent powers of endless growth to lift the soul to its high destiny,—surely while every mind must bow reverently and humbly before the greatness of the christian life, every heart must exult at the thought of the aim above and the power within.

"Blessed be the God and Father of our Lord Jesus Christ, who according to His great mercy begat us again unto a living hope by the resurrection of Jesus Christ from the dead, unto an inheritance incorruptible, and undefiled, and that fadeth not away, reserved in heaven for you, who by the power of God are guarded through faith unto a salvation ready to be revealed in the last time . . . . having been begotten again, not of corruptible seed, but of incorruptible, through the word of God, which liveth and abideth."

"Choose well; your choice is
  Brief, and yet endless."—*Goethe.*

"Others I doubt not, if not we,
  The issue of our toils shall see;
  Young children gather as their own
  The harvest that the dead had sown,
  The dead, forgotten and unknown."
                              —*Clough.*

"A wonderful thing is a seed!
  The one thing deathless forever;
  The one thing changeless, utterly true;
  Forever old and forever new,
  And fickle and faithless never.

"Plant virtue and virtue will bloom;
  Plant ill and ill will grow.
  You can sow to-day; to-morrow will bring
  The blossom that proves what sort of thing
  Is the seed—the seed you sow."

"One base deed, with prolific power,
  Like its cursed stock, engenders more."

"Blood for blood and blow for blow,—
  Thou shalt reap as thou didst sow.
  Age to age with hoary wisdom
  Speaketh thus to man."—*Aeschylus.*

THE LAW OF THE HARVEST.

"Be not deceived; God is not mocked: for whatsoever a man soweth, that shall he also reap." (Galatians 6: 7.)

This is the law of the harvest. Everything that hath life carries within itself the principle of its own existence, that which determines the method by which it develops and the end for which it lives. Whatever may come from without to modify or change the life, must act through its principle of life; and, although this modification or change come by some command, or law, it must act in harmony with the law ruling within. Ought we to draw so broad a distinction as we usually do between the law written in our hearts and the law given to us by revelation? Both are given of God, have the same work and purpose, and are mutually corroborative. One of the first exercises of an awakened conscience is to testify to the truth of God's revealed law, and of the awakened heart to respond in penitence and prayer to God's infinite love. This correspondence between the two expressions of God's law for human life is clearly indicated in this law of the harvest.

A field produces according to the seed beneath its surface, and the fertility of the soil. The same law holds good in every soil, whether in the physical, intellectual, or spiritual world. The whole world is busy sowing and growing for a future harvest. In the physical world, how eagerly the germ of life within the seed bursts its bonds and strives to reach its appropriate harvest. All the various forms of vegetable life multiplying themselves many fold, a single seed dying to produce its many successors for the autumnal ingathering. The animal world, by increase and dispersion, is taking possession of every part of the earth, while men and their brute servants are ever urging the vegetable world to a more vigorous development to support the rapidly increasing animal life.

In the intellectual and moral world, how eagerly men are sowing for the future reaping. Thought-germs of every kind and in every form of utterance are striving for growth towards the harvest. In lecture, book, sermon, newspaper, conversation, in the very look of the face and the shrug of the shoulders, men are busy sowing and cultivating. Parents and teachers are diligently scattering seeds for growth in soil more valuable and productive than any that farmer ever ploughed, and out of all this seed the final harvest of the child's life shall be gathered.

Every human soul is entrusted with soil, seed, and opportunity for the required harvest. Your life-soil is fertile, endures forever, and is forever your own. You cannot sell it. You cannot rent it. You can mortgage it only to sin, whose certain foreclosure is death. The seed may be as immortal as truth from God, or deadly as satanic error. The opportunity is all your life, with its wealth of resources, its innumerable calls of duty, and its wide opportunity for truest growth and noblest work.

The law of the harvest is simple and certain. According to the kind, quality and quantity of the seed sown, the fertility of the soil, and the amount and quality of labor bestowed on the sowing and the cultivation, so shall the harvest be.

The Apostle starts out with the warning, "Be not deceived; God is not mocked." Do not deceive yourselves into thinking that you are deceiving God. No formal service that is heartless, no crying "Lord, Lord, have we not done wonderful things in Thy name?" when the spirit is dead, will deceive Him who looketh upon the heart. And yet is there not a general hope, certainly a wish, that God may count what little good we have done, as some sort of atonement for what we are? What is this but expecting Him to take our occasional good deeds, and draw from them a permanent good character.

We cannot expect Him to violate His own laws of life in order to save us from the appropriate results of our neglect or wilful disobedience. God does not have special cases. Every germ of life produces after its kind, according to a perfectly definite law of development. This law, so forcibly stated by the Apostle, contains several particulars.

Whatsoever a man soweth, *that* shall he also reap. As the seed is in *kind*, so must the harvest be. The sower must choose his harvest in his choice of the seed. A man who sows to the physical life shall reap a harvest for the physical life. One who sows all his seed for the intellectual life shall reap the intellectual harvest. In like manner, one who sows to the spirit shall reap a spiritual harvest. You have the power to choose which of these you will sow, but you have no right to expect that you may sow one kind of seed and reap another kind of harvest.

Your power of choice lies with the seed; you cannot change the law of the harvest, which must be as the sowing. You may sow but one kind of seed, or mingle all good seed in proper proportion; but whatsoever you sow that shall you reap.

All good is arranged by the Apostle in two classes, temporary good,—"He that soweth to the flesh shall reap corruption;" and permanent good,—"He that soweth to the spirit shall reap life everlasting."

Each after its kind.

The two classes have many things in common and many resemblances, but in kind they are as different as earth and heaven, as temporary and everlasting. Both may be ours, for we get what we sow for. A man may sow to the spirit, without being blessed with physical comfort. And because he has sown abundantly of the choicest spiritual seed is no especial reason that he should be prosperous in his physical life. To have both, he must sow for both.

Christ says, "Blessed are they which do hunger and thirst after righteousness: for they shall be filled." What with? Righteousness. Just as those who hunger and thirst after this world's prosperity shall be filled with that. Each class gets what it seeks. "Honesty is the best policy" for this life and that which is to come, but that is not saying that the honest man will get rich, or keep free from disease and sorrow. A man may be a good man and get rich, or he may be just as good and remain poor. Or a man may choose to get rich and have all the comforts of this life, without a thought of the everlasting life.

"Abraham's bosom," heaven, was the legitimate harvest of the seed sown by Lazarus; but he had no more right to expect that he would receive the home and the luxury which the rich man enjoyed, than the rich man had to expect heaven as the harvest of his life. Each got what he sowed for.

A man cannot sow to worldly success only, and have any right to expect a spiritual victory, a victory over death. "He that soweth to the flesh shall (from that sowing) reap corruption," and corruption is only another name for death, the end of all flesh. Every man must sow for the harvest he wants. The student who would become a learned man knows that he must sow years of self-denial, and close, hard study. He has no right to complain of his harvest of ignorance and inefficiency if he has never sown the seeds from which a richer harvest could grow.

You have no right to complain that although you are a devoted Christian, serving God with fervent spirit, yet your neighbor, who cares for nothing but his own success, is growing rich and influential, while you are hardly able to pay your just debts. You sowed for peace of mind and all the christian graces here, and eternal life in the world to come. Your neighbor sowed for worldly success. You are both getting what you sowed for. If you want wealth and influence, you must sow accordingly. The Master said of the hypocritical Pharisees, whose very religious services were performed for the praise of men, "They have their reward."

They sowed for the praise of men and they got it.

The man who sows for worldly success has a right to expect worldly success, but he has no right to expect anything else. If the Christian expects to have worldly success because he is a Christian, he misinterprets God's law of cause and effect. What a man sows, he shall reap. He cannot expect a harvest of physical comfort from a sowing of spiritual seed. Incidentally, the spiritual growth will help the growth of all true good, even physical good; but the seed must be planted for every part of life's harvest.

But, some may say, there is a difference between the spiritual law of growth and the physical, in this that God loves the sinner, and nature does not; God forgives sin, and nature does not. Because God is love shall He violate laws which are altogether good and pure, laws which are the most perfect expression of His love, as of every other attribute of His nature? His love is deep as eternity, mighty as omnipotence, broad and rich as human need, and helpful as the Christ himself; but that love is shown in the perfect *fulfillment* of law, not in the violation of it. Christ "came not to destroy the law, but to fulfill." And the divine love was displayed as much in the atoning death as in the obedient service.

God's law of command never violates His law of principle, for what He speaks in revelation is in strict harmony with His utterance in the inherent, abiding principles of man's moral nature.

Suppose you have a young almond stock and want a harvest of apricots, how will you secure the change of fruit? You will graft an apricot stem into the almond stock, and the fruit will be apricots. Thus you change the harvest by changing that which produces it. But then I read in this book of God that it is no exception to this law, or violation of it, that God forgives sin, but in strictest accordance with it. "Ye must be born again." The seed is changed in order to change the harvest.

The law is that a seed can produce but one harvest, and that the harvest shall be of the same kind as the sowing. You may choose to sow either to the flesh or to the spirit, but you must not expect to gather both the physical and the spiritual harvest from one sowing.

Many of you are young, and you often hear this exhortation, but has it no meaning that it need not be repeated? You are sowing seed with a free hand in very productive soil—what shall the harvest be? The answer is plain—exactly what the seed was. Do you think that you can sow any kind of seed now, and then reap in later years any harvest you may wish?

There is in a distant state a man whose life is full of good works. He wears to the world a cheerful face, and helps every life he meets. But there is a load on his heart that only the redemption of his body can remove. He did a great wrong in his youth. After his conversion he made every reparation in his power, but it was too late to remove all the harm, and the sorrow of that memory goes with him through life.

Say what you please about what a man ought to do, how he ought to feel at peace when he has done everything in his power to repair his wrong, and by a penitent, humble and devoted life is doing all he can to help others. The law of God and the law of nature,—if you can thus separate two methods of the same law—require that every harvest shall be as the sowing. And though a man may be born again, he cannot forget the old life, with its joys and its remorse, until the new life has swallowed up in its ever-increasing abundance all the past, and swept even its memories clean.

The sins of youth are sure to produce some harvest. God forgives, and plants the seed of a new spiritual life, but He does not enable you to forget. And one mark of this new life is its power to deepen the soul's remorse for sin, even while it increases the longing for righteousness. We have no right to expect that in later years we shall reap the harvest of honest speech and candid mind, when we filled our youth with insincere words and uncharitable thoughts. Not only will the *reputation* earned in youth cling to us but the habits of thought and tone of spirit will influence and modify our characters to the end of life. The most fearful of all dangers to an immortal soul is that doom which Christ said had fallen upon some who heard the Parable of the Sower, "their heart is waxed gross," they had lost their capability for any higher life. We forget that "God requireth that which is past," because we forget that there is no past with God, and fail to remember that nothing dies, and that everything produces its own harvest. Remember the timely warning of the wise preacher in Ecclesiastes, 11: 9: "Rejoice, O young man, in thy youth; and let thy heart cheer thee in the days of thy youth, and walk in the ways of thine heart, and in the sight of thine eyes; but know thou that, for all these things

God will bring thee to judgment." It is the same law; as thou sowest thou shall reap.

Neither does God with His forgiveness send any new power to the body to escape the harvest of the earlier sowing. You may have become a true child of God, but if your youth has been spent in indolence, idleness and dissipation, you will feel the loss of power to the end of your days. Not only so, but if a man in early spring-time sows a crop of thorns, he will not only gather no good crop, but he is thus far weakened by loss of time and skill and opportunity when he would be very glad to sow a better seed. Many people who wish to "do good" after their days of business and youthful pleasure are over, find that they have lost their aptitude for it; sometimes have lost even their capability for work so different from what has busied them in all their earlier years. They sowed one kind of seed, and they must not expect to reap another kind of harvest. The old Latin proverb urges that "you must become an old man when young, if you would be a young man when old;" suggesting that you must apply the temperance and wisdom of maturity to youthful inclinations, if you would preserve the strength and vigor of youth to old age. As Pope puts it—

> " For fainting age what cordial drop remains,
> If our intemperate youth the vessel drains?"

Many of us who are yet young would repudiate our future selves with all the zeal and loathing of Hazael of old, should some Elisha make that future plain to us.

We shall reap as we sow, and yet sometimes people (not thoughtful people) say that if one is only sincere it matters little what a man believes. Wheat and rye look very much alike to one who is not familiar with them, but suppose a farmer, honestly believing that he is sowing wheat, actually scatters rye broadcast over his field, will he get a crop of wheat for his honesty? A man will get what he sows—whatever he may think he is sowing.

There is one fallacy in our reasoning

about goodness that needs to be noticed. The goodness which Christ teaches and what is called the world's goodness, or moral goodness, are different in kind. The fruits bear a close resemblance. Indeed, the world's highest morality is a harvest of our Master's sowing. Our noblest view of life and our highest conception of God come from Christ's life and teachings. Yet there are men who deny Christ, and yet want to claim God as their Father. They say, perhaps, that science has taught them this view of God. Yet science tells us very little about God, except that He exists and is all-powerful. These men take the view of God which Christianity has taught the world, and proclaim it as a discovery of their own skill and knowledge. Christ's own answer to all such is given in St. John 8 : 42 : "If God were your Father, ye would love Me: for I came forth and am come from God." But whatever their view of God, and however they may have received it, there is a difference in kind between the "moral life" and the spiritual, and the final harvests must bear the same difference. These men are entitled to all the reward of a true morality, with all it means of health and comfort and good influence. But they have no right to expect that their earthly life, beautiful as it is, will grow to a harvest in God's likeness. They have sowed the seed of the highest earthly life, and they shall reap accordingly, but the harvest will be no higher or more enduring than the sowing. It is still "sowing to the flesh," and only he who sows to the spirit shall reap "life everlasting." The one is living by earthly motives, according to an earthly standard, and must always measure himself by the lives of men like himself. The other is moved by heavenly motives, according to a divine standard of life, and always measures himself by the perfect life of Christ, God's ideal life for man. One life is guided by custom, and controlled by external influences. The other is guided by the principle of a new-born life within, and controlled by a divine spirit to whom he has surrendered his life. The "moral life" has its life and reward this side of death, for the grave is the end of its growth. It is a beautiful and fruitful earthly plant, soon reaching maturity and death, but its seeds reproduce only in an earthly soil. The spiritual life never reaches maturity on earth, but requires a spiritual world for its fullest growth. It aims to bring forth all the good fruits of the "moral life" as a legitimate harvest of its own life on earth, but looks for a still higher fruitfulness in an unending world. The "moral life" touches no higher power than its own, supported by the pressure from without of forces that are altogether earthly. The forces that control such a life rarely touch the mass of men, and have at best only a reforming power, and that is chiefly negative. These forces come into a life with all the prohibitions of the law, but with none of the gospel of a new life. It commands the life to put forth its own greatest power, but it gives no new power. The moralist is one who tries to live up to the standard of morals reached by the world under the influence of Christianity. The Christian is one in whom Christ has begotten a new life, which is lifting him by steady growth towards perfection. One may be a reformed man, but the other is a regenerated man. One life is the fruit of earthly seed, and the whole growth will be as the seed, earthly. The other life is growing towards an eternal harvest from a divine seed of God's own planting. The one is begotten of the best spirit of the world, the other is born of the Spirit of God. Each after its kind shall reap a harvest, but the two harvests will be as different as the sowing.

Prof. J. C. Shairp, in his "Studies in Poetry and Philosophy," uses the following strong and suggestive language: "Character, which, when regarded from a merely moral point of view, almost inevitably becomes a building up from our own internal resources, takes altogether another aspect when it is seen that true character is in the last resort determined by the attitude in which the spirit stands to God. Then it comes to be felt that the rightness men search for cannot be evolved from within, must go beyond self, must fall back on a simple receptivity, receiving the rightness and the right-making power, which they have not in themselves, from out of the great reservoir of righteousness which is in God. Only on thus falling back on God, and feeling himself to be, as of everything else, so of righteousness, a recipient, is a man truly rightened. Thus the last moral experience and the first upward look of religion agree in one, 'A man can receive nothing except it be given him from above.'"

Again the harvest must be as the sowing in *quality*. After a man decides what kind of grain he must sow in order to secure the kind of harvest he wants to reap, he is careful to select a good quality of that kind of grain, for he knows that the quality of the harvest is affected by the quality of the seed. A good farmer, when he has decided to sow wheat, seeks to get for his seed the best quality of wheat in the market; and the student, when he has decided to study any particular theme, seeks to find the ablest teachers and most helpful books, so that by the best methods and the best quality of seed he may be sure of a good quality of harvest. So it should be in the spiritual sowing. It is needful for us all to have the choicest spiritual seed, if we would have the richest spiritual harvest. This seed is the word of God. The words of men may be wise and very helpful; but every Christian knows that the power to sanctify is the word of truth. The faith that enables us to receive aright the blessings of God, "cometh by hearing, and hearing by the word of God." For this there is no safe substitute. Nor must the *quantity* be regarded as an unimportant matter, for if one wants to reap bountifully, he must sow bountifully. No farmer is so ignorant as to do on his farm what so many intelligent and cautious people do in the spiritual work of their lives; sow as little as possible, and yet hope to reap a very great abundance. Sowing to the flesh a hundred dollars for every dime they sow to the spirit; sowing a week's work to the flesh for every hour they give to spiritual work; sowing a thousand fold for the body over the handful they scatter for the spiritual harvest. As they sow in kind and quality and quantity, so shall they reap.

Another particular of this law is that of *increase*. You plant a single grain and it gives you in return a score like itself. Your harvest is not according to the labor and money you expend upon it. These alone do not give the full value of the product. The natural fertility of the soil, and the ability of the seed to multiply itself so abundantly, must be considered. This power of multiplication, the seed has in itself; but there is another mode of increase that must not be overlooked, that by *diffusion* or *dispersion*. Whether it be thistle-down floating on the air, the lady-slipper exploding to scatter its little seed-bullets, or the seeds of trees and grass and grain carried by the wind, or the birds, or on the bosom of flowing waters, far and wide the life is dispersed to grow and multiply in new lands. Everyone recognizes this law in nature, every student knows how true it is in the intellectual life, and the word of God says, as we have seen in the Parable of Growth, that it is as true in the spiritual life. You cannot keep either spiritual good or evil from increasing. The good we do and the evil we do go on producing their harvest to the end, multiplying and diffusing their influence, each after its kind. One would think that no exhortation could be needed to make us cautious in our every word and deed in presence of such a responsibility. But we are apt to forget the wisest admonition, grown familiar by its frequent repetition, even as we are apt to overlook the greatest values in things grown customary by our constant use of them.

"To do good and communicate, forget not, for with such sacrifices God is well pleased." "Herein is my Father glorified, that ye bear much fruit." These, to one who seeks to "sow to the spirit," are not mere commands, but are the very principle of his life. They are commands of duty, but they are eagerly accepted as in perfect harmony with his own new-born spiritual life, and the grain does not more eagerly accept the sunshine and the rain for its growth to the harvest than does the earnest Christian accept these commands and the opportunities they give for growth towards the final harvest of his own full-grown and ripened life.

By a different emphasis, we may learn another lesson, which is also suggested by the first sentence of the Parable of Growth. "Whatsoever a man *soweth*, that shall he also *reap*."

Every true life is one of activity. No man drifts to real success, for while he may suddenly and without effort secure possession of great wealth or high position, he has not that discipline of self which comes with the labor of achievement. In no department of life does one gather a good harvest without a previous sowing. Hence the work, the manner of its performance, and the spirit of the worker, all enter into the life-problem of every human soul. And this is true, not only in the great affairs of life, but also in every little thing. For everything, whether great or small, is both a seed and a harvest, the seed for future growth and the fruit of a previous sowing. Contempt of littles may be contempt of the greatest values, for we never know how much of growth may lie within the smallest seed. You cast a little word of truth into a young heart, and never knew that from your sowing there sprang up great principles to control an immortal life. Nor did you see the many seeds that have fallen from that life to spring up and grow in other souls unto endless life.

A divine spirit makes everything divine that it touches, and a consecrated spirit consecrates every work it performs, whether the world call it small or large. As Mrs. Gaskel's "Ruth" expresses it:

"There is a right way and a wrong way of setting about everything—and to my thinking, the right way is to take a thing up heartily, if it is only making a bed. Why, dear, ah me! making a bed may be done after a very christian fashion, I take it, or else what's to come of such as me in heaven, who've had little enough time on earth for clapping ourselves down on our knees for set prayers."

Any man is great who does all his work for the spirit and the duty in it, who feels that each lowly task may be so performed as to help the noblest spiritual growth. Religion "put on" is a very deadly thing, like the famed shirt of Nessus, putting the wearer to a miserable death. But religion that springs from the heart, and flows naturally with consecrating power into every walk of life, is a very noble thing, making the life beautiful in all abiding graces, and "fruitful in every good work." But such a life comes not by accident. Its own appropriate sowing and its own natural growth must precede it. Evil crops grow without any care, but good seed must be sown and carefully cultivated. All plants and trees producing food for man are short-lived, and require constant care to prevent their degeneration. Even the famous breadfruit, which we once thought did not come under this rule, is no exception to the law; for of the two varieties of the breadfruit-tree, the wild propagates itself, and is worthless for food, while that which yields food is seedless, and requires constant care for its growth.

In the spiritual world, the very labor of sowing and cultivating enters into the quality of the fruit, and prepares the soul for the proper enjoyment and use of the harvest. The great purpose of the activity to which Christ urges his followers is to crowd out the evil growth by the more abundant sowing and cultivation of the good. "Sow beside all waters," however weed-grown and stony, for it is thus that Christ would "destroy the works of the devil." Indeed, the Master would teach us to measure our life less by the number of its years than by the spirit of its service and the abundance of its fruits. How can any soul accustomed only to reaping, without a thought of sowing, ever rightly appreciate the self-denial and never-resting service of Christ? What can he understand of the joys of Him who delighted to do God's will, and of the heaven that rewards the faithful steward, when he is a stranger to the spirit of devotion to the work of ministering unto others? The Saviour's admonitions concerning hearing might well be applied to sowing; take heed *how* ye sow, and take heed *what* ye sow. Before sowing, decide what you will sow, and that will be decided by what you want to reap in the harvest. And do not overlook the fact that this law applies to every part of life.

To public life and to private. To the school and the church, to the store and the home, to politics and to business.

If you want to reap success in business, you must sow accordingly; but remember that you may be so "diligent in business" (or in house-keeping, or in study) as to become unable to "be fervent in spirit." Perhaps you say, "I will first be successful in business, and then with my wealth I will serve the Lord with all faithfulness." Nay, if you do not continue "fervent in spirit, serving the Lord," while you are increasing you wealth, you will never properly unite them afterwards. Much of the devotion to business which the world applauds is the very process that is destroying spiritual growth. Many of our business men, pressing forward eagerly for wealth, need to consider this law of life which God has written in such unqualified language.

Ask yourselves whether, when you shall have secured possession of wealth, you will be richer or poorer than now? You will possess much, but will you *be* more or less than now? Be watchful, lest you choke your spiritual life, God's harvest, with the too abundant growth of your own earthly harvest! "It is required of stewards that they be found faithful." Not only when they have laid by all that they want for themselves, but from the first moment of life.

Every moment this law is in full operation in every life, yet do we not often try to make ourselves believe that its action is not certain, or at least that it is far off in the future? We treat life as if it were a mere succession of acts and thoughts and words, when these are but the leaves and blossoms and partial fruits of a life which is unbroken and endless. Thinking that we can at any moment cease to perform the acts, we forget that they are but expressions of a life steadily growing to a harvest from the sowing of all the past. For all life is an unbroken series of beginnings, as well as of harvests. The slight inclination, which we may have inherited, may seem to us a very small matter, yet from it may grow a wish, an affection, an act, a habit, all doing their part in shaping and establishing our character. How careless we are of the seeds that fall into our lives, and the lives of those for whom we are responsible! We pay so little heed to the sowing, but when too late to destroy the evil, and cultivate the good to advantage, we curse ourselves for our folly, and plead for God to pity us. We are apt to think of retribution as something which belongs exclusively to a distant future and another world, yet every soul carries within itself the prophecy of its own judgment. For retribution is implied in every threat of conscience, and illustrated in every controversy between good and evil for the control of the will. In every temptation, the will is solicited by opposing feelings, and we can do no more than to choose the best or the worst that is before us. If we choose the worst thing, is it not the wickedest thing we are able to do at that moment? It is no palliation to say that others have done worse things than we ever have, for they did no more than the wickedest thing that lay within their reach, and that we have done. We know that in every temptation there is a choice between two things, and these two things are not of equal moral worth, so that we are ever choosing either the best thing or the worst. Thus we are ever casting the seed for a future harvest, habituating the will to obey the purer affections in its decisions, and quickening these affections to more vigorous growth; or putting the will more and more under the control of the evil in us, and thus determining our characters away from good and from God.

We know that neither good nor evil receives its full retribution in this world; every life's experience is proof of that. Conscience punishes the most spiritual with the keenest remorse for sin, while it speaks but feebly in those who dwell in crime. But the law abides forever; "whatsoever a man soweth, that shall he also reap." "Even as I have seen, they that plow iniquity and sow wickedness, reap the same." (Job 4: 8.) What a fearful meaning this gives to that last proclamation of this same law: "Seal not up the words of the prophecy of this book; for the time is at hand. He that is unrighteous, let him be unrighteous still: and he which is filthy, let him be filthy still: and he that his holy, let him be holy still. And behold I come quickly; and my reward (wages) is with me, to give every man according as his work shall be." (Rev. 22: 11, 12.)

Solemn and threatening as this law may be in one direction, it is full of comfort and encouragement in another. A sower of good seed has only to look at the wonderful growth of "the word of the kingdom," to see how certainly this law applies to good as well as to evil. It will make him penitent for the evil he has done, but it should make him diligent and hopeful in every faithful service of good.

Diligent, to make the future sowing

both good and bountiful. Hopeful, for the harvest shall be as the sowing, for every good seed carries within itself the decree of its own certain growth to the final harvest, and is guarded and nourished by the blessing of "the Lord of the harvest."

Every seed is a beginning; if the seed be true and good, it is the beginning of blessings that cannot die. For your own soul, for your children, for all lives that feel you influence, have seeds of blessing ready in the abundant fruitfulness of your own life. Remember "the Sower," who never came in contact with human life without leaving some seeds of comfort, or warning, or hopefulness, never counting any too low or too great to receive the word of life. There is no better life for this world or heaven than His, "who came not to be ministered unto, but to minister."

"Wherefore, be ye steadfast, unmovable, always abounding in the work of the Lord, forasmuch as ye know that your labor is not in vain in the Lord."

"Now He that ministereth bread for your food, multiply your seed sown, and increase the fruits of your righteousness."

"Now the God of peace, who brought again from the dead the Great Shepherd of the sheep with the blood of the eternal covenant, *even* our Lord Jesus, make you perfect in every good thing to do His will, working in us that which is well-pleasing in His sight, through Jesus Christ; to whom *be* the glory forever and ever. Amen."

SOWING AND REAPING.

Sow with a generous hand;
    Pause not for toil or pain;
Weary not through the heat of summer,
    Weary not through the cold spring rain;
    For the sheaves of golden grain.

Scatter the seed and fear not,
    A table will be spread;
What matter if you are too weary
    To eat your hard-earned bread.
Sow while the earth is broken,
    For the hungry must be fed.

Sow;—while the seeds are lying
    In the warm earth's bosom deep,
And your warm tears fall upon it,
    They will stir in their quiet sleep;
And the green blades rise the quicker,
    Perchance, for the tears you weep.

Then sow;—for the hours are fleeting,
    And the seed must fall to-day;
And care not what hands shall reap it
    Or if you shall have passed away,
Before the waving cornfields
    Shall gladden the sunny day.

Sow; and look onward, upward,
    Where the starry light appears,—
Where in spite of the coward's doubting
    Or your own heart's trembling fears,
You shall reap in joy the harvest
    You shall have sown to-day in tears.

—Adelaide Procter.

A PRAYER FOR THE HARVEST.

Oft as Thy word, O God, is cast,
   Like seed into the ground,
Let the rich dews of heaven descend,
   And righteous fruits abound.

Let not the ever watchful foe
   This holy seed remove,
But give it strength to root and grow,
   And ever fruitful prove.

Let not the world's deceitful cares
   The living word destroy,
But may it, free from hindering tares,
   Bring forth life's purest joy.

O speed Thy message here to-night
   To every listening soul;
And fill each heart with heavenly light,
   And strength to reach life's goal.

The seed is Thine, and Thine the power
   To give it great increase,—
O send us now a gracious shower
   Of faith and love and peace!

www.ingramcontent.com/pod-product-compliance
Lightning Source LLC
Chambersburg PA
CBHW020826230426
43666CB00007B/1109